Lernthriller Englisch

Die Genetische Falle

Story: Susi Weichselbaumer
Übersetzung: Stuart Vizard

Compact Verlag

Bisher sind in dieser Reihe erschienen:

- Compact Lernthriller Englisch Grammatik
- Compact Lernthriller Englisch Konversation
- Compact Lernthriller Englisch Grundwortschatz
- Compact Lernthriller Englisch Aufbauwortschatz

In der Reihe Lernkrimi sind erschienen:

- Compact Lernkrimi Deutsch Grammatik
- Compact Lernkrimi Deutsch Grundwortschatz
- Compact Lernkrimi Englisch Grammatik
- Compact Lernkrimi Englisch Konversation
- Compact Lernkrimi Englisch Grundwortschatz
- Compact Lernkrimi Englisch Aufbauwortschatz
- Compact Lernkrimi Französisch Grundwortschatz
- Compact Lernkrimi Italienisch Grundwortschatz
- Compact Lernkrimi Spanisch Grundwortschatz
- Compact Lernkrimi Spanisch Grammatik

Weitere Titel sind in Vorbereitung.

Chefredaktion: Evelyn Boos
Redaktion: Brigitte Stoffel
Fachredaktion: Lynda Hübner
Produktion: Wolfram Friedrich
Titelillustration: Karl Knospe
Typografischer Entwurf: Maria Seidel
Umschlaggestaltung: Carsten Abelbeck

ISBN 3-8174-7569-1
7275692

Besuchen Sie uns im Internet: www.compactverlag.de

Vorwort

Mit dem neuen, spannenden Compact Lernthriller können Sie Ihre Englischkenntnisse auf schnelle und einfache Weise vertiefen, auffrischen und überprüfen.
Agent Hunter erleichtert das Sprachtraining mit Action und Humor. Er und seine mysteriösen Fälle stehen im Mittelpunkt einer zusammenhängenden Story.
Der Thriller wird auf jeder Seite durch abwechslungsreiche und kurzweilige Übungen ergänzt, die das Lernen unterhaltsam und spannend machen.
Prüfen Sie Ihr Englisch in Lückentexten, Zuordnungs- und Übersetzungsaufgaben, in Buchstabenspielen und Kreuzworträtseln!
Ob im Bus oder in der Bahn, im Wartezimmer, zu Hause oder in der Mittagspause – das Sprachtraining im handlichen Format bietet die ideale Trainingsmöglichkeit für zwischendurch.
Schreiben Sie die Lösungen einfach ins Buch!
Die richtigen Antworten sind in einem eigenen Lösungsteil zusammengefasst.

Und nun kann die Spannung beginnen …

Viel Spaß und Erfolg!

Inhalt

Story

Agent Peter Hunter ist ein alter Hase im Geschäft. Ob im In- oder Ausland, wann immer es gilt, das Verbrechen zu bekämpfen – Hunter ist zur Stelle und riskiert Leib und Leben. Unter seinen Kollegen beim Britischen Geheimdienst gilt er als Einzelgänger. Der Erfolg bei seinen Operationen gibt ihm Recht, auch wenn Hunter oft nur haarscharf dem Tod entrinnt.

Mysteriöse Sterbefälle häufen sich in England und greifen dann auch auf andere europäische Länder über. Handelt es sich um eine Seuche? Einen terroristischen Akt? Was haben die Fertignahrungsmittel einer britischen Firma mit all dem zu tun? Verbotene Genmanipulation?

Der Geheimdienst setzt seinen besten Mann auf den Fall an: Hunter. Unterstützung bekommt er diesmal von der jungen Biologin Agnes Westcombe. Die „graue Labormaus" hat jedoch wenig Ahnung, was es heißt, als Agentin unterwegs zu sein. Sie muss schnell lernen, denn Hunter und sie befinden sich plötzlich in einem Verwirrspiel, das ungeahnte Dimensionen annimmt. Skrupellose Verbrecher verschleppen die beiden nach Amsterdam. Jetzt hängt ihr Leben am seidenen Faden ...

The Genetic Trap

Tina rushed along the brightly lit hospital corridor beside the stretcher. The walls were painted white. The linoleum floor reflected the grey light from the neon lights on the ceiling. There were silver handles on the white doors and plastic signs next to them. The printed letters on the signs went past so fast that you couldn't read them. She was running as if her sister's life depended on it.

While she was running, she held her sister's hand, which was unnaturally cold and felt like wax. Tina's eyes were fixed on Nancy's face. Her eyes were closed and her mouth was a thin red line in her white face. Her black eyebrows stood out unnaturally and made a strange parallel to the horizontal line of her mouth.

Nancy's chin pointed upwards. A cord ran along both sides of her neck. "They must be the arteries," thought Tina, and she wanted to stroke her fingers over them to help Nancy to relax. But she couldn't let go of her sister's hand. She continued running and holding her hand tightly. "Or am I holding myself tightly?" Tina wondered.

The bright white sheet over Nancy's chest was hardly moving. "Breathe," Tina whispered to the colourless face. "Stay with me, stay with me!"
She repeated these words quietly over and over again. The right leg of her jeans rubbed against the metal bars which stuck out a little from under the mattress. She found the hardness pleasant, like a support that was directing her and the two doctors in the only possible direction.

Übung 1: Wie heißen die Körperteile auf Deutsch?

1. head ____________________
2. back ____________________
3. leg ____________________
4. forehead ____________________
5. eyebrow ____________________
6. cheek ____________________
7. throat ____________________

Suddenly, a silver swing-door appeared. Two nurses in green uniforms came out and held open the doors. They waited until the doctors had pushed in Nancy's stretcher. They looked quickly at Tina. The fatter nurse with round pink cheeks nodded slightly. The taller and thinner one looked right through Tina. "Thank you," Tina wanted to say, and, "Please help her." But she couldn't say a word.

"Excuse me," said a man's soft voice beside her. "Are you related to the patient?" asked the young man. He was about 1.70 metres tall and his eyes were at the same level as Tina's. They were warm and brown. His hair was uncombed. In his white nurse's coat and his well-worn trainers he looked a bit like a little boy who had borrowed his father's big shirt for an art lesson to protect him from the paint. "Are you an acquaintance, a close friend, her sister?" he asked again, looking her directly in the eye.

"Sister," she answered. She thought her voice sounded strange. It was hoarse and quiet, as if it came from somewhere very deep or very far away. Tina saw everything around her like through a mist.

She stared at her feet. "I got home and Nancy was in the bathroom. I could hear her. She was being sick. I went straight to her. It was all over the place, the floor, the toilet, everywhere. Then came the blood. So much of it. It just didn't stop coming out of her mouth. Then she choked and I held her and screamed and tried to stop the blood with a towel. But there was just so much." Here she stopped. The short round nurse with the rosy cheeks was standing in front of her holding a dark brown plastic cup under her nose. She could smell weak tea with powdered milk from a vending machine. The cup was steaming. "Careful, it's hot," the nurse warned.

"Thank you," said Tina, taking the drink. Her eyes caught the nurse's. She wasn't wearing the operating uniform anymore, but a white nurse's uniform instead. The healthy pink of her cheeks had become much paler.

"Drink it," she told Tina.

"What's wrong with my sister? Where's Nancy?" she interrupted.

"Drink it," the nurse said again.

Übung 2: Finden Sie das passende Gegenteil!

1. fat ______________________
2. quick ______________________
3. sad ______________________
4. tall ______________________
5. weak ______________________
6. thick ______________________
7. hot ______________________

ÜBUNG 3 !

Übung 3: Setzen Sie die richtigen Präpositionen ein!

The cold wind bit into Hunter's face. His nose was red and poked 1. _______ of his scarf. It was late evening. Ice was already building up on the road. He went quickly 2. _______ the tube station 3. _______ the block of flats on the outskirts of London where he had lived for a few years. He ran up the steps of the small staircase to his door.

In the corridor he took 4. _______ his gloves and rubbed his hands together.

"That's how you know a business man!" Edwin Jones, the caretaker, laughed. The old man was mopping the floor. It seemed Hunter wasn't the only tenant who had walked into the entrance hall with dirty shoes that evening. Jones looked disapprovingly 5. _________ the wet footprints he had left 6. _________ the tiles. To distract attention from what he had done, Hunter carried 7. _________ with Jones's opening remark.

"You're right. We in the finance department are like Scrooge. Always piling up and counting the money." He carried on rubbing his hands together and walked past Jones smiling. The caretaker believed – like everyone else in the building – the cover that the secret service had arranged for Hunter.

People believed the agent was an employee in the finance department of the London City Council. As long as there was no power cut, it was actually a rather nice cover.

The agent entered his flat and took off his coat and scarf. He immediately took a ready-meal from the fridge. While he was freshening up in the bathroom, the macaroni and cheese was cooking in the microwave. A "ping" from the kitchen told him the food was ready. He opened a bottle of beer. Then he sat down to dinner in front of the television. He was happy with himself and the world. He had now been back in Operations for three weeks and was finally finished with the office duty he had been forced to do a few weeks before.
He toasted the candidate on the television show with his beer. As he scraped off the burnt layer on top of the pasta with his fork, the face of Callaghan, his boss, flashed across his mind. She had known since his last case that he knew of her corrupt activities and involvement in illegal arms deals. It was also quite clear to her that he had no hold over her and no proof at the moment.
"Not yet," said Hunter out loud to the quiz show presenter, who was just announcing the commercial break.
"I'll get you one day, Doctor Helene Callaghan!" he added. Until that happened, he was just happy for every action-packed new day. "Finally in Operations again!" he said happily. He bit into a steaming macaroni and burnt himself on the hot food. The pain in his tongue went all the way down his throat.

Übung 4: Wie heißt der Beruf auf Englisch?

1. Polizist ______________________
2. Lehrer ______________________
3. Sekretärin ______________________

4. Anwalt ______

5. Zahnarzt ______

6. Hausmeister ______

A cheerful noise met him when he entered the open-plan office the next morning. He had been assigned to his old unit, the "5th Rapid Response Unit" under Captain Martens. So his desk was again in the office which he shared with the twenty other agents in the group.

Next to him sat Percy Horn, his new assistant. Yet again today this very ambitious young man was at his desk before Hunter. He seemed to be busy sorting through the drawers of the filing cabinet. He had pulled out the filing cabinet from under his desk and he was looking through files, cards, bits of paper and pens.

"Good morning!" said Hunter

"Oh, er, good, er, good morning, sir!" he stuttered. Hunter's arrival had surprised him and he added, "I didn't hear you come in."

He stood up to his full height. He was 1.95 metres tall and so towered 10 centimetres above Hunter. Unlike Hunter, who was slim and muscular, Percy was very thin. He looked more like a young teenager who had grown too quickly than a man in his late twenties. Everything about him was too long and thin.

ÜBUNG 5 !

Übung 5: Setzen Sie das Verb ins Simple Past!

1. go ______

2. come ______

3. watch ______

4. see ________________

5. find ________________

6. have ________________

7. enter ________________

"Isn't this nice and cosy," said a woman in a brown suit. Her jacket was tight around her. Her shoulder pads made the top part of her body look a little blown up.
"I didn't hear you come in," said Hunter this time. Percy interrupted him saying, "Good morning, Mrs Callaghan."
"Dr Callaghan," she corrected him sharply. Her eyebrows rose a little. Her blue-grey eyes took on a cold, steely look.
"How long have you been in the Rapid Response Unit?" She looked sympathetically at Hunter. "Or should I say back in the Rapid Response Unit?"
Hunter stood up in front of his boss, who was taller than he was.
"Three weeks," he replied, then added with extra emphasis, "Dr Callaghan." She smiled at the last words with her deep red lipstick-covered lips. Standing with her hands on her hips, she pushed her chest forward. She looked directly at Hunter. But before she could reply, he quickly said:
"To what do we owe the honour of your visit?"
He realised he had emphasised this last sentence a little too much. The way she looked told him that his remark had amused her.
"You know very well that I'm especially worried about you, Hunter," she said, flatteringly. "I just want what's best for you. After the trauma in Italy. But let's put that behind us. The girl is dead and buried now and we can't do anything about it. Although, wouldn't you like a picture of her? Your desk looks rather empty."
A smile flashed across her lips. Hunter swallowed hard but said

nothing. Percy sniffed. Hunter couldn't stand this habit the young man had and shouted, "Don't start with that!"
"Sorry," he mumbled.
Callaghan smiled. "If you're so eager to do something, Hunter, I've spoken to Captain Martens. I'd like to take you out of the Rapid Response Unit for a special case."
Hunter did not react and waited.
"A case which is very close to my heart." She paused dramatically. She tilted her head as if she was trying to assess Hunter again before giving him the job.

ÜBUNG 6 !

Übung 6: Übersetzen Sie!

1. gemütlich ______________________
2. unterbrechen ______________________
3. mitleidig ______________________
4. Lippenstift ______________________
5. Schreibtisch ______________________
6. besorgt ______________________

He wondered how her turban of brown hair stayed in place. She must use a ton of hairspray to keep it in place. His looking at her hair seemed to irritate her. She said quickly:
"The Public Health Department has contacted us. A girl died suddenly last night." She said it in the same relaxed tone that she had just used to talk about Gina, the girl in Italy.
"Probably from some kind of food poisoning," she added.
"So just a routine check then," said Hunter in conclusion.
"You could say so, Agent Hunter. But as the secret service it is our

duty to investigate in such circumstances. An unknown cause of death. The patient died in a public hospital. It was probably an allergic reaction. That's usually the key to things like this."
Hunter nodded. So did Percy.
"Here are the files," said Callaghan, as she passed Hunter a pile of papers in a folder. He took them from her quickly.
"Now don't look at it so disappointedly. You shouldn't underestimate routine checks. There's a lot to do for a hard-working agent. And who knows, you might come across a big mystery in there."
At this point she laughed. So did Percy.

Übung 7: Welche Wörter haben eine ähnliche Bedeutung?

1. answer	☐ pause
2. say	☐ need
3. give	☐ telephone
4. stop	☐ reply
5. want	☐ speak
6. call	☐ end
7. cry	☐ pass
8. finish	☐ shout

They had heard it a dozen times before at the Academy – you should always try to avoid these routine checks which various offices gave you from time to time. If you got one to do, you could be sure that you would spend three or four weeks without a break sitting at your desk filling out forms, requesting reports, filling out more forms, chasing up other reports …
The young man suddenly choked and started to cough violently. Hunter looked at him angrily. Percy tried to bring the coughing

under control. Annoyed, Hunter turned back towards Callaghan. Still laughing, she said:

"Oh yes, Hunter. I'm afraid you can't count on the active support of our young friend here for this job." For the first time in the conversation she spoke directly to Percy: "Horn, you're going to the training camp for as long as Hunter is busy with the allergy case. You'll have enough time. After that, you'll remain Hunter's partner in Operations under Captain Martens. You'll be able to see what action in the field is like. You should be happy. You're leaving tomorrow."

She turned quickly. "That will be all," she added. Without turning round again, she made her way to the door.

Percy shrieked with delight. He was looking forward to the training camp. An agent had so much to learn and he had only very recently finished his basic training in the Academy and started in the service.

When he noticed how unhappy Hunter looked, he suddenly felt sorry for him.

"I'll send you a postcard," he said timidly. "I'm sure it'll be exciting for you, with the dead girl and all that."

ÜBUNG 8 !

Übung 8: Bringen Sie die Sätze in die richtige Reihenfolge!

1. worked secret Hunter the for service.

2. in happy he work Operations to was.

3. had he there few lived a years for.

4. more wanted Percy learn job to his about.

____

5. sad girl he dead Italy was the was in.

____

6. knew Callaghan's activities about he illegal.

____

At about 7pm Hunter left the office. Most of the others had already gone. Emmerson had said he was sorry about the "stupid job" Callaghan had given him. But before Hunter could thank him for the sympathy, Emmerson was already on his way out with three other colleagues. The four of them made up a special commando which was going to Paris next week. That evening they had been given their equipment from the arms store and shown how to use everything they were taking with them. That had made Hunter very envious.

It was always great fun trying out all the newly developed weapons and spy equipment. And also, when you were in the top secret and maximum security laboratory in the cellar, there was always the chance of seeing one of the prototypes which were still in the test phase. Marvin Brenner and his men and women were always willing to bend the secrecy rules a little to present their new achievements to anyone who was interested.

"Don't think about it," Hunter told himself. How could he have believed that his transfer back into Operations would happen so smoothly? How could he have believed that Callaghan would let him off the leash so easily and so soon? He felt happy that his suspicions about her corrupt dealings had at least made her respect him.

ÜBUNG 9

Übung 9: Übersetzen Sie folgende Sätze!

1. Hunter war sehr neidisch auf Emmerson.

2. Er teilte das Büro mit zwanzig anderen Kollegen.

3. Callaghan trug dunkelroten Lippenstift.

4. Sein Beruf war strengstens geheim.

5. Ich schicke Ihnen eine Postkarte!

His neighbour, Rosi Carpenter, met him at the entrance to the flats. She invited him to dinner at her flat, which she shared with her five-year-old daughter Ginny. Hunter apologised:
"I'm already busy tonight."
They agreed on the following evening – dinner at Rosi and Ginny's in their attic flat.
Hunter really did have something planned. He had decided to start investigating the suspicious death right away. In his flat he changed his clothes, deciding on light-coloured trousers, a dark-coloured shirt and a leather jacket. He used a little hair gel to tidy up his greying hair. Then he left the flats.
He drove into the city in his estate car. It was almost half past ten when he finally found a parking space. Despite the cold, the streets

in Chelsea were not completely empty. A few girls were hanging around the display cases of a boutique which had models dressed in strange fantasy uniforms.

Hunter had not been in London's artists' quarter for a long time. A few things had changed in the last couple of years. The shops had become more commercial and the prices had risen. Hunter wondered if the antique market with all kinds of colourful bric-a-brac, and which was regularly held in the King's Road, brought a little of the old flair back to the streets.

The cold of the winter night bit through his leather jacket. He walked faster. The bar had to be somewhere nearby.

A thin blue beam of light from above lit up the sign with its old-fashioned writing which said "Empire" and hung over the wooden door. He went in. Gentle jazz music surrounded him. The air was smoky.

Übung 10: Bringen Sie die Buchstaben jeweils in die richtige Reihenfolge!

ÜBUNG 10 !

1. TIVENI (einladen) ______________

2. TLEHARE (Leder) ______________

3. ONBRIHGUE (Nachbar) ______________

4. PLAOSEOIG (sich entschuldigen) ______________

5. WSMEOHREE (irgendwo) ______________

6. TMQPEINUE (Ausrüstung) ______________

He decided to sit on an empty stool at the bar and asked one of the waiters in white uniforms for the cocktail list. While he pretended to read it, his eyes moved around the room. He looked at his watch. It was just before eleven; she had to appear any moment now. He knew her from a photo.
"Tina, the most beautiful barmaid of all, the queen of the shaker," one of the waiters said to her when she arrived. She was also wearing a white uniform. Her blond hair was tied in a ponytail. The mouth in her pale face stretched into a smile.
"Hello, chief, everything all right in the bar?"
Hunter's plan was simple. He wanted to talk to her in a relaxed atmosphere. He put on his most charming smile.
"Excuse me, I'd like a Bloody Mary."
At these words her face twitched. He realised his mistake. Just a few days ago her sister had died and he wanted a "Bloody Mary".
It seemed that tonight just wasn't his night. The bar filled up with more and more people. Tina was so busy that he could hardly say a word to her. He decided just to watch her. Maybe he could catch her after work.
Tina was leaning over the bar at the other end when Hunter saw something silver flash. A man grabbed her by the ponytail and pulled her head right back. She quickly looked at the customers. She gave a crooked smile as if to say "this is only a bit of fun".
The man in the dark suit had broad shoulders. His head sat squarely on his thick neck. The silver thing was a knife, Hunter saw. The attacker placed the end on her throat directly under her chin. Her hands clenched around the edge of the bar.
"Hey!" shouted one of her colleagues and rushed over to Tina and the stranger. In a flash the man removed the knife from Tina's skin. Before the waiter had reached the young woman, the stranger had already disappeared.

From where he was sitting, Hunter could not hear what the two of them were saying. But a few seconds later he saw Tina nodding in agreement. The waiter put his arms around her and held her a moment. Then the girl left her post behind the bar.
Hunter jumped down from the bar stool and rushed after her but he quickly lost her in the crowd of people.

Übung 11: Markieren Sie! Richtig ✔ oder falsch –?

! ÜBUNG 11

1. In der Bar saß Hunter an einem Tisch. ☐
2. Es war kurz vor halb zehn. ☐
3. Hunter bestellte Bloody Mary. ☐
4. Tina hatte kurze Haare. ☐
5. Der Angreifer drohte Tina mit einem Messer. ☐
6. Tinas Kollege griff den Mann an. ☐
7. Der Angreifer konnte entkommen. ☐

"The staff entrance!" Hunter suddenly thought. He pushed his way through the crowd and out of the wooden door into the fresh air. A few metres down the street there was another door – an inconspicuous metal door. The bell had "Empire – Office" on it.
The agent turned the handle. But the door was locked. With an expert hand movement he brought a bunch of lockpicks out of his trouser pocket. He tried two or three. Finally one fitted. Before he could turn the metal bolt in the lock, the door was pushed open. As quick as a flash, he sprang aside.
"Oops!" he said cheerfully.
"Sorry, I didn't mean to kill you with the door," joked Tina weakly. Without looking at him, she walked past Hunter down the street. The metal door locked behind her.

Not knowing what to do, the agent hesitated a moment. How should he speak to her? He saw that she was making for the driver's side of a car.

"Stupid old car," she shouted angrily and kicked the car door. "Bloody old heap. Bloody day. Bloody everything!"

Hunter rushed over to her. "Can I help?" he asked.

"Damn it …" She stopped suddenly. "Yes, please. My key won't fit in the lock!"

Hunter looked closely at her face which was framed by a fur hat. She recognised him. "Oh, the Bloody Mary," she said.

He smiled and repeated his offer of help.

"I don't understand." The girl's voice was still high-pitched, almost hysterical. "I locked it when I went to work. Now I want to go home and I can't unlock it."

She poked around in the lock with her key.

"Are you sure it's your car?"

She answered sarcastically, "No, I always try to steal other people's cars and I can never understand why my key doesn't fit the lock."

Hunter stayed calm. "It's quite cold tonight. Let me see. Maybe your lock's frozen. Have you got any de-icer?"

She wanted to started shouting again, but suddenly shrugged her shoulders in resignation under her thick coat. "I'm sorry. I'm Tina. Thanks for helping me."

! ÜBUNG 12

Übung 12: Was gehört zusammen?

1. staff	☐ oven
2. machine	☐ floor
3. car	☐ deal
4. ground	☐ phone

5. shop ☐ camp
6. microwave ☐ entrance
7. arms ☐ stool
8. bar ☐ key
9. mobile ☐ assistant
10. training ☐ gun

Hunter rattled the door handle. The old Fiat shook and creaked. The driver's door didn't move an inch. The agent tried the key Tina had given him on the passenger side. It didn't work there either.

"I'm Peter," he said. "Maybe we should try it in daylight. Or you? Maybe you should try it tomorrow when it's light. You can hardly see it in the dark like this. It seems to be frozen solid."
"Oh please try it once more," she begged him.
"I'm afraid I don't have any de-icer in the car either."
"What about with this?" she said, passing him a lighter.
"Great!" said Hunter and lit the flame. The bright light blazed along the lock. He put the key back in the keyhole. This time the lock sprang open.
"You're my hero!" she cried enthusiastically. "I work in the "Empire" on Thursdays and Sundays. The next time you come I'll give you a free drink. Even a Bloody Mary!"
Tina laughed and gave him a kiss on his cold cheek. Then she climbed into the car through the door Hunter was holding open for her.
"Good night, Peter!" she said.
He said goodbye with, "See you soon!" and slammed the door shut. She slid onto the driver's seat and struggled to take off her coat.

Übung 13: Setzen Sie die richtige Präposition ein!
(at, on, in)

1. ________ Tuesday
2. ________ 1998
3. ________ three weeks
4. ________ the 1990s
5. ________ 7.30 pm
6. ________ 19th June
7. ________ Christmas

Hunter went back along the street to the front of the "Empire". On Sunday his chance would come. The case wasn't that urgent; he could wait until Sunday. To see Tina again. To find out about her sister's death. Maybe even to ask her a few other things.

He strolled further along the street to his car.

"Hunter, she's in her mid-twenties," his moral conscience reminded him.

He heard the diesel engine of the little Fiat start after a couple of attempts. The regular spluttering of the engine mixed with the rhythm of his heartbeat. Sunday wasn't far off.

All of a sudden a loud explosion rang through the night. Several loud bangs followed and bits of metal fell down hard onto the concrete. Hunter had thrown himself to the ground and rolled away from the shop window, behind one of the cars parked in the street. He heard a crackling and popping. When things had settled down, he stood up slowly. He could now hear loud voices and steps running along the street. A man shouted, then came several more voices.

Hunter stared in the direction he had come from. He began to run, faster and faster. He stopped suddenly. From here he could see it. There was hardly anything left of the little Fiat after the explosion. Flames jumped out of the remains of the car. Like a strange ruin, they rose up towards the night sky in the glowing light of the fire.

Übung 14: Setzen Sie die Wörter an den richtigen Stellen ein!
(bundle, bunch, crowd, loaf, pack, pint, queue)

1. a ________________ of keys
2. a ________________ of bread
3. a ________________ of beer
4. a ________________ of papers
5. a ________________ of cards
6. a ________________ of people
7. a ________________ of traffic

Who might have wanted to kill Tina? The question preoccupied Hunter for the whole of the next morning. He sat at his desk staring at the tabletop.
"Excuse me?" His thoughts were interrupted. The words came shyly from the thin lips of a delicate-looking girl. She wondered if she might have disturbed Hunter somehow.
"Maybe I should come back later. Or some other time?" She began to move away.
"Wait, wait!" Hunter said to stop her. She turned back to him awkwardly. She had short black hair which was thick and slightly wavy

around her head. She wasn't wearing any make-up. In the bright light of the office lights it made her look very pale. She couldn't be older than in her mid-twenties, Hunter guessed.
"What can I do for you?" he asked politely.
"Westcombe, Agnes," she said quietly.
"Sorry?" said Hunter. The word came out as if it had been fired from a pistol.
"Westcombe, Agnes, sir, biologist in Section 3, Dr Wander's Laboratory Unit. Specialising in microbiology and genetic research. Previously military, now secret service." Her mouth closed quickly and her shoulders rose and bent forward slightly.
"I've been assigned to work with you because of the job from the Public Health Department."
Callaghan had a strange knack of assigning him female colleagues, thought Hunter. He said out loud: "Well, Westcombe, Agnes. Find yourself a chair and we'll discuss what's going on here."
She looked at him, unsure. "Westcombe, sit," he tried, a little more brusquely.
"Yes, sir!" she answered quietly. Then again louder: "Yes, sir!"
Hunter sighed and watched her.
She put down her chair and apologised for taking so long.
"That's all right," Hunter interrupted.
"Yes, sir!"
"And can we please stop the 'Yes, sirs'. We're not in the army here."
"Yes, sir. Yes. Sorry." She fell silent again, remaining in her unnaturally upright position. It was no use, the woman was a complete nervous wreck.
The conversation with the biologist gave Hunter nothing of interest. The only new thing was that there had been other similar deaths in the meantime. And the first ones on the Continent.

Hunter sent the girl back to the laboratory. She was to check the findings of the Public Health Department, then meet with the secret service Pathology Department. Hunter thought it best for her to re-examine the bodies of Tina's sister and some of the other new arrivals.

Übung 15: Ordnen Sie jedem Wort sein Gegenteil zu!

1. loud	☐ bent
2. interesting	☐ dim
3. ordinary	☐ shy
4. bright	☐ relaxed
5. polite	☐ boiling
6. best	☐ strange
7. upright	☐ quiet
8. confident	☐ rude
9. tense	☐ boring
10. freezing	☐ worst

ÜBUNG 15 !

That day he left the secret service building in the centre of London a little earlier than the day before. The building was in the banking district and was disguised as a large bank and financial consultancy. He pulled his coat tighter around himself when he got into the cold winter air. The few metres to the underground station would be enough for him.

"No sudden moves," a muffled voice ordered behind him. He wanted to turn his head but something was being pressed hard into his back. It had to be the barrel of a gun.

"Be a good boy and keep walking in front of me. Don't try to turn around." Hunter obeyed. He walked slowly forwards. The streets were almost empty of people at that time of day. The man walked close behind him.

"What …?" Hunter started to ask.

"Shut up …," shouted the man.

At that moment the agent quickly turned around and ducked. The huge man fired. The bullet missed Hunter by an inch. Quickly he kicked the man hard. The man fired at him again. Hunter's kick to his knee had made him stagger and again the shot missed its target. The man found his balance again. He was bigger than Hunter and was wearing a dark suit. His round head on a thick neck seemed familiar to Hunter. With all his strength he hit the man under the chin.

The man's head was knocked to one side, but he found his balance once again. He hit Hunter with a crack on his shoulder with the butt of the gun. The agent groaned loudly. He gave the man another kick. The karate kick to his wrist hit exactly the right place. The gun fell from the man's hand and he screamed loudly. He bent down to pick up the pistol. The agent gave him a karate chop from above. The big strong man fell flat out onto the concrete.

Hunter dashed over to the gun and picked it up. A car came screeching around the corner. The window was wound down and a driver's voice thundered:

"Ted, you idiot!" Shots were fired through the window. One scratched Hunter's arm. A sharp pain passed through him. He dropped to the ground like a flash and rolled over the cold wet concrete. He crawled on hands and knees behind a bin on the pavement. He used it as cover and he fired at the car.

In the meantime one of the men had got out of the car. He lifted his accomplice off the ground, dragged him to the open car door and manoeuvred him onto the back seat. Hunter fired and hit him in the leg.

"I'll show you," he growled. His upper arm was still burning.

He raised his head above the bin to fire again. Before he could aim, a bullet landed in the metal of the bin just under his neck. He ducked as fast as lightning.

The car roared off while its passengers continued to fire at Hunter. He stayed down and repeated the car registration number to himself over and over again. He only stood up as soon as the sound of the tyres had disappeared into the distance. He took a notebook out of his coat pocket and calmly wrote down the letter and number combination of the registration.

"I'll get you," he swore to himself.

Übung 16: Beantworten Sie die Fragen zum Text!

ÜBUNG 16 !

1. What did the Secret Service building look like from the outside?

2. Where was Hunter going when the attacker put a gun in his back?

3. How did Hunter escape from the man?

4. What was the attacker's name?

5. Who shot Hunter's arm?

The evening at his neighbour's was pleasant. She had made lamb with mint sauce. Ginny was allowed to help, but decided to prepare her own food. So there was lamb with mint sauce and Ginny-style chips.

Rosi was sorry to hear that Hunter had hurt his arm on the filing cabinet. He had bandaged the wound and lied about his injury.

Because of the special occasion, Rosi had put candles on the table. She looked for some matches for a few minutes but couldn't find any. Hunter came to the rescue. He fished a lighter out of his pocket. He looked at it in amazement before passing it to Rosi. He had no idea that he had put that lighter in his pocket.

It was the one he had got from Tina. The word "Mealomeal" was written in pink letters on a yellow cover. Rosi laughed when she read the word.

"You poor bachelor. You have to eat microwave ready-meals all the time, eh?"

Because Hunter was staring at her uncomprehendingly, she explained: "Mealomeal's a company that makes ready-meals for the microwave. Now don't tell me you didn't know that." She laughed again.

"I think they've only been around for a few months. Apparently they're very successful. Our supermarket already has a whole section just with "Mealomeal" products."

"Amazing," said Hunter.

Rosi paused for a moment. "Like all of these companies, they're all helped along a bit to increase sales."

"What do you mean?" the guest asked.

"Well, you must know as a ready-meal eater. Most of them use genetically-modified food for their products. Genetically-modified soya, for example. Or vegetables. They grow faster, are more resistant to pests, they're bigger and cheaper to produce …"

Ginny interrupted her mother. "What's getenically-modified?" Rosi smiled at her daughter's mistake. Without waiting for an answer, Ginny suddenly asked:
"Finished?"
"What?" said Hunter, startled.
"Thanks!" cried the child and pulled his full plate of chips over to herself.

Übung 17: Sind diese Wörter richtig ✔ oder falsch – buchstabiert?

! ÜBUNG 17

1. aparently ☐
2. bachelor ☐
3. successfull ☐
4. advantage ☐
5. consultancy ☐
6. vegtable ☐
7. lighter ☐

Later, Rosi took Ginny to bed. Over a cup of espresso, she continued chatting to Hunter about the advantages and disadvantages of single life, then they moved onto other subjects.
It was already eleven o'clock when the agent went back to his flat. The door was not locked, but that didn't surprise him. It sometimes happened that he forgot to lock it when he visited a neighbour. Especially when his thoughts were elsewhere. To be exact, when he was thinking about a blond girl who had been blown up in her car. In the flats everyone knew everyone else. And on the ground floor, Jones saw everyone who came and went.
Without switching on the light in the hall, Hunter went straight into the kitchen. Here he turned the light on over the kitchen table and

began to search through the freezer compartment. He took out all of the packets of microwave meals he could find. The pile on the table was enormous, he had to admit. He looked at the company names on the boxes. There was only one from "Mealomeal".
Indian-style chicken curry. He turned the cardboard box in his hands.

Übung 18: Bilden Sie die Gegenteile mit dem richtigen Präfix!
(dis-, im-, in-, un-)

1. lock ______________________
2. agree ______________________
3. experienced ______________________
4. polite ______________________
5. possible ______________________
6. cover ______________________
7. comfortable ______________________

Two iron fists grabbed him from behind. Hunter had not heard anything and was now choking desperately. The grasp was stopping him from breathing. He tried to kick, but his foot hit nothing. The intruder was holding him too far away. The man's thumbs were boring deeply into Hunter's throat. His lungs were ready to burst. He needed air.
He hit out wildly with the frozen box in his hand. He didn't know where to aim for. He was trying desperately to breathe. Black spots appeared before his eyes. He head felt as if it was swelling like an air balloon. His opponent swore at him: "Keep still, you bastard!"

Hunter carried on striking out. He swung the box around once again. This time it hit against something.
The swearing immediately stopped. The grip around Hunter's throat loosened. He threw the cardboard box to the floor and massaged his neck with both hands.

Übung 19: Lesen Sie weiter und unterstreichen Sie die englische Übersetzung der folgenden Wörter!
(1. Atemzug, 2. zusammengebrochen, 3. kniete, 4. schluckte, 5. Schubladen, 6. schrie)

He drew a deep breath of air into his lungs. It felt good. It took a few moments before he could breathe naturally again. Hunter turned around. Crumpled on the kitchen floor lay the big strong man that Hunter had already met. The agent knelt down next to him. He felt for a pulse in the man's neck. He pulled back his hand in disgust.
The man was dead. He stared up at Hunter through wide-open eyes. A wound gaped open at the side of his head, with pieces of skin hanging off, bleeding a little. The solid frozen box must have hit him directly at that point.
Hunter swallowed.
He heard steps in the corridor. He didn't hesitate for a second. In one expert movement he squeezed past the dead man and ducked under the table. His hands were shaking as he opened one of the bottom drawers of the kitchen cupboard which stood next to the table. He armed himself with a carving knife and quickly slid back under the table.
The steps were getting nearer. Two people entered the room. Hunter could see their heavy boots. A woman screamed.

"Shut up!" her companion ordered. He then said, "Come out, little Hunter. Come out. We're Tina's friends and we didn't find it very nice that you had to watch her and her car go up in smoke."

Hunter stayed quiet. He knew his hiding place was obvious. In fact, when the two of them dragged the dead body of their colleague to one side a little, the woman said,

"Is that our good little boy sitting under the kitchen table?"

With his pistol drawn, her companion bent down towards Hunter. He was directly in front of the table. The agent still waited. The man fired. The shot rang out loudly in the silence of the kitchen. Hunter had moved quickly out of the way. He rammed the knife with all his strength into the man's leg. His scream mixed with the bang of another shot. Again the gunman missed.

The man in the black suit was still pointing the gun at Hunter, who slid further under the table.

! ÜBUNG 20

Übung 20: Bilden Sie aus den unten angegebenen Adjektiven und Verben die passenden Substantive!

1. strong ______________
2. happy ______________
3. silent ______________
4. mix ______________
5. die ______________
6. amaze ______________

Hunter grabbed the handle of the knife with both hands. He pulled it out of the wound. The injured man screamed fiercely. Blood streamed from the deep cut. The man crawled towards Hunter and forced him against the kitchen cupboard. The agent held the carving knife in front of his face.

The intruder aimed his pistol directly at Hunter's head.

"Help me!" he screamed to his partner.

She then began to crawl under the table. She didn't have enough room in the narrow space.

"Look out!" her colleague growled over his shoulder. This second was enough for Hunter. He hit out at the man's wrist with his left hand. The man was surprised, cried out and dropped the gun. As he moved towards Hunter again, the woman was shocked by the scream and at the same time tried to get the second pistol which had slid in her direction.

The shot from her gun sounded muffled. Her colleague groaned: "Are you crazy?"

Blood came out of his mouth as he said it. He wiped his lips with his sleeve and looked at the blood.

The woman became hysterical. She fired again, scrambled out from under the table and ran away. If her first bullet had hit the man by mistake, her second one was clearly aimed.

Her colleague was still shocked by the blood from his mouth. His body had twitched once when the second bullet had hit him. He coughed violently and spat out. Blood and leftover food hit Hunter. He couldn't escape it in the small space he was in. Everything ended as quickly as it had begun. The man coughed violently again, then his body fell forward limply.

His well-built figure fell onto Hunter, who was still holding the knife. He now let it drop. With both hands he pushed the body off him and hurried to the door. The woman was nowhere to be seen. The light was out on the staircase. He went back into the flat.

He felt sick as he cleaned his face and hands quickly on a towel.

From his living room window he looked down onto the street in front of the flats. Further off, he saw the red back lights of a car disappearing around the corner towards the city. It was not worth chasing anymore.
He sighed as he dialled the number for the secret service. All this would make Callaghan very angry with him. Risking his cover because of a shoot-out in his own home.

Übung 21: Finden Sie ein sinnvolles Synonym für die Wörter in Klammern!

1. He (washed) ______________________________ his hands.
2. His boss was very (annoyed) ____________________ with him.
3. The attacker (fired) ______________________________ at the agent.
4. You have to be (mad) __________________________ to jump out of a plane.
5. Hunter (rushed) ________________________________ to his car and followed his attackers.

The clean-up team had finished their quick and professional work while it was still night. The bodies had been taken away in blue plastic bags with "bulky rubbish" written on them. Even the lorry which they put the bags into had "Bulky Rubbish – Service Round The Clock" written on the side. No one noticed anything.
When Hunter left the house the next day, he met Jones. The caretaker was in the middle of changing a light bulb. While he was

moving the ladder out of the way to let Hunter go past, he asked him, "Could you turn your TV down next time. Why were you watching a Western so late at night? All that loud shooting!" Hunter already had the door handle in his hand while the other man continued, "It's not for me. It's for little Ginny Carpenter – do you think she can sleep with all that noise? If you really want to be good friends" – here he winked – "with upstairs, then …" Hunter said dryly, "Thanks. I'll watch a cartoon tonight then." Before the caretaker could decide whether to laugh or get angry, the agent had already left.

Übung 22: Welches englische Wort wird beschrieben?

1. The part of your body between your hand and your arm.

____

2. The letters and numbers on the front and back of a car.

____

3. The part of a lamp which lights up.

____

4. The part of a door you use to open it with your hand.

____

5. A person you work with.

____

6. The person you live next door to.

____

An envelope was waiting for him on his desk. The result of the check on the car registration was that the car belonged to a private security firm.

“Security firm?” he growled. “They’re more like a danger firm!” There was also a list. It gave the names of various companies which specialised in security. There were a lot of unknown names underneath. His secret service colleague who had done the check had done a very good job.
He had found out that over two thirds of the names on the list were not real companies. The rest really existed. One of them was “Mealomeal”, with its headquarters in Birmingham.

“I’ll pay them a visit tonight, then,” thought Hunter. But what was he actually looking for?

*Übung 23: Welches Verb ist richtig – **make** oder **do**?*

1. ______________ an appointment
2. ______________ your homework
3. ______________ the shopping
4. ______________ a mistake
5. ______________ a good job
6. ______________ the washing-up
7. ______________ some exercise
8. ______________ a decision

Determined footsteps approached his desk. They were accompanied by strained greetings from the agents who shared the open-plan office with him. Even before Callaghan had appeared in front of him, Hunter knew what was coming:
"Hunter! What was all that about last night? You kill an entire football team in your place and we're supposed to clean it up? Or how is it that there were two men in suits stone dead in your flat? You're under cover in that block of flats if you understand what that means!"
Callaghan stopped to take a breath. Hunter let a few moments pass. He wanted to wait for her to get everything off her chest.
"What you're doing isn't just some unimportant little job for the Public Health Department!" she said coldly. "In the meantime we have 26 victims in England alone. All of them singles or young people. All of them dead around lunchtime or dinnertime. The symptoms are always similar to food poisoning. Vomiting, blood, death. Germany, Holland, and France have also reported similar cases."
Hunter had stayed calm the whole time. Now he explained: "I have a good lead – it points directly to "Mealomeal". And I'm going to follow it up tonight and get a couple of samples from their laboratories."
Callaghan was dumbfounded for a moment. She pulled at her jacket. "Well, let's hope that you're on the right track."
She paused nervously. "Where's Westcombe?" she asked.
Hunter had not seen the strange girl since their first meeting.
"Take Westcombe with you and examine the samples there. I don't want you drawing any more attention to yourself like last night. You're not an amateur!"
"Thanks for the compliment," Hunter replied. "I like hearing things like that!"

She stared at him furiously through screwed-up eyes. Without saying another word, she turned on her heel and left.
She hurried to the door amid the hesitant goodbyes of the others in the office. Hunter smiled.

Übung 24: Übersetzen Sie!

1. Mittagessen ______________________
2. Labor ______________________
3. ähnlich ______________________
4. seltsam ______________________
5. sich übergeben ______________________
6. ruhig ______________________

His smile disappeared, though, when his colleague at the desk to his right waved a postcard at him.
"Hey rookie! Lots of love from the holiday camp!" Hunter mumbled something and took the card out of Emmerson's hand. The front was completely black except for the yellow words: "Kent by night". He studied the back.
"Dear Agent Hunter, I hope you're well and you're getting further with you research. You've probably found out in the meantime where I am." At this sentence Hunter paused for a moment, stunned, then read further.
"You were right, a whole new world opens up once you know what could happen to you out there. I had no idea. I don't think I can say what. Everything's top secret here. Best regards, your assistant Percy Horn."

"I have no idea what could happen to you," Hunter repeated to himself. Agnes Westcombe had no idea what would happen to her, either! Spontaneously, he decided to forget about the plan to break in. How could he get into the building unnoticed with her? She was a lab assistant, not a secret agent! He called her and explained the situation. She agreed to each of his instructions with "Yes, sir!"

Übung 25: Welches Wort hat eine ähnliche Bedeutung?

1. disappear
   - a) ☐ grab
   - b) ☐ vanish
   - c) ☐ crawl

2. research
   - a) ☐ profession
   - b) ☐ hobby
   - c) ☐ investigation

3. stunned
   - a) ☐ shocked
   - b) ☐ angry
   - c) ☐ tired

Agnes was late. She arrived at his desk shortly before four. She had visited a supermarket to buy "Mealomeal" products. Then she had tested the contents of each packet in the laboratory.

"Some of the tests still need a bit more time," she reported to Hunter. She then sat down on the chair she had brought with her without being told to by him.

Hunter said nothing. He would never have believed she had so much initiative.

"That sounds hopeful," he said confidently. A glance at "Kent by night" made up his mind.

"Agnes, we have two and a half days until we act. Tomorrow, Wednesday, and half of Thursday."

He continued quickly so that she could not start saying "Yes, sir" again.

"We'll now get you a special operations suit and equipment for the job. You know yourself what stuff you'll need for the lab. Early tomorrow morning we'll start with the practical side. We'll meet at Regent's Park tube station. Leave the station at the front of the train and take the left exit outside."

Now that he had finished she could have said something. He would even have accepted a "Yes, sir". But she stood up in silence. She got hold of the chair by the back to take it back to where she had found it. With a quick glance at the agent, she signalled to him to lead the way. Then she lowered her head again.

"Earth to Westcombe, Agnes!" Hunter said to himself. He took the lead. Agnes placed the chair back behind Emmerson's desk. Together, Hunter and Westcombe moved towards the door.

"Have you got a moment?" asked Captain Martens, who met them at the door. He drew Hunter to one side. "Hunter, I need you from the middle of next week for a very important mission in the Pacific. I want you to take it over. It needs a loner. Make sure you've finished all this routine nonsense for Callaghan by then. You know that when the boss speaks, even Captains have to obey."

He patted the agent knowingly on the shoulder. When he noticed Agnes, his lips moved strangely. He smiled at the agent encouragingly. His hand was no longer on Hunter's shoulder but was touching her lightly.

Übung 26: Setzen Sie die richtige Form des Simple Past ein!

An early morning mist (1. to hang) ________ over the streets when Hunter (2. to leave) ________ the underground station. It (3. to be) ________ just before seven and he was shivering. The Bakerloo line had been full of people. In his running shoes, tracksuit bottoms and fleece pullover, he had stood out from the others who were travelling to work dressed in their suits, uniforms and overalls.

From time to time he (4. to jump) ________ up and down and (5. to wave) ________ his arms about. He (6. to rub) ________ his gloved hands together and (7. to pull) ________ his woolly hat further over his ears. Running in winter (8. to be) ____________ apparently unhealthy and bad for the lungs. But he (9. to want) ________ to test Agnes's condition first without any spectators before he (10. to go) ____________ on the machines with her in the secret service fitness rooms.

"I hope she doesn't arrive in her special operations suit," he thought. He had forgotten to tell her that when she had got her suit. Those things were only supposed to be worn during a mission; they were very expensive and very conspicuous if worn during the day or where there were other people. He still found it strange that she had taken the suit, weapons, and equipment without question. He was going to show her how all the stuff worked later that afternoon.

"She'll never make a good agent," he concluded. He was cold. The mist was slowly clearing and the outlines of the trees in the park were becoming sharper. He jumped up and down on the spot again and spun his arms around in the air. Someone came up behind him and started imitating his movements.

ÜBUNG 27 !

Übung 27: Wie heißt das Wort auf Deutsch?

1. expensive	☐ Selbstvertrauen
2. conspicuous	☐ ausgeleiert
3. outline	☐ teuer
4. mist	☐ beschleunigen
5. muffled	☐ auffällig
6. confidence	☐ Lauftempo
7. baggy	☐ Abriss
8. accelerate	☐ ermutigend
9. pace	☐ Nebel
10. encouraging	☐ gedämpft

Hunter suddenly felt stupid and stopped abruptly. Agnes stopped too and looked at him hesitantly.

"Good morning," he said.

"Morning," she answered.

"Shall we start?" Hunter asked. He didn't know what to talk about with her.

"Yes, sir," she snapped. She was wearing basketball boots and a baggy grey tracksuit.

She had pulled the hood of her top tightly around her face. The girl irritated him. He was even more irritated because it seemed she had a bulging rucksack on her back. "Strange!"

First he jogged at a medium pace around the Inner Circle of the open-air cinema, then they took the Outer Circle around the park and the agent increased the pace. Agnes was always just behind him. She did not seem bothered by any of it.
He stopped. He jumped powerfully over a fallen tree on the ground, over and over again. She watched him. Yet again he felt he was making a fool of himself. He stopped jumping. Instead he waved his arms around quickly.
Agnes had been running on the spot next to him the whole time. She now lined up behind him and both of them started jogging again.
After two hours Hunter thought it best to stop running. He had to admit he was exhausted. Sweat was running out from under his hat over his face and the T-shirt under his fleece pullover was sticking to his back. He took a shortcut and sprinted along the narrow path between the bushes back towards the tube station. When he saw the sign he threw his arms up and sighed with relief.

Übung 28: Unterstreichen Sie das „schwarze Schaf"!

ÜBUNG 28 !

1. irritate, encourage, anger, annoy
2. look, peer, watch, bother
3. rough, tough, delicate, hard
4. drive, sprint, rush, dash
5. tired, exhausted, baggy, weary
6. hood, belt, cap, hat
7. steering wheel, windscreen, mirror, gun

Everything was quiet behind him. He looked back along the path, but he couldn't see Agnes anywhere. He quickly ran back and

looked everywhere for her. The bushes at the edge of the park there were thick.
As he came out of the thicket he suddenly saw her. Someone was following her close behind. Judging by the tall, broad figure, it had to be a man. He was dressed in dark clothes. He was pushing the girl in front of him to the other side of the park.
Hunter chased after them. He took out his gun and followed them at a safe distance. One time the man turned round. Hunter quickly had to hide behind a park bench. Agnes and the stranger reached the end of the park. He pushed her roughly into a black car. He forced her to sit next to him on the back seat. The car drove off.

ÜBUNG 29 !

Übung 29: Unterstreichen Sie die richtige Alternative!

Hunter did not (1.) lose/miss a second. He rushed out of the park. He (2.) smashed/broke into a car that was (3.) placed/parked at the side of the road. He (4.) pulled/fiddled with the wires under the steering wheel. The car (5.) started/began. He (6.) jumped/forced himself quickly into the slow-moving traffic. The stopping and starting frustrated him. He had to try hard not to lose the black car. Someone (7.) played/sounded the horn aggressively behind him as he (8.) changed/turned lanes without indicating. They slowly (9.) entered/reached the edge of town. Here, the traffic was moving more freely. He (10.) pushed/accelerated to get behind the car which was turning into a dual carriageway.

Hunter should have chosen a faster car. He soon saw that the distance between him and the black car was getting bigger. He pressed the accelerator until it touched the floor. But it was no use, the car could not give any more.

He knew that what he had planned was risky. He also knew there might be trouble. But he did it anyway.
He waited for the moment when there was no car between his and the one with Agnes in it. The electric window whirred. He only had one chance. His hand shook slightly as he fired.
"Damn, the gap is still too big," he thought. A fraction of a second later a bang broke the tension. One of the tyres of the car he was chasing had burst. The car went into a spin and skidded into the crash barrier. It then bounced off it, back into the road.
Hunter braked. Car horns sounded behind him. A car shot into the second lane to pass him. There was a loud crash as it rammed the first car. Another car overtook Hunter and collided with the first.
Hunter stopped in front of the accident. A traffic jam was already building up. With his gun drawn, he crouched behind the stolen car. He looked carefully over the edge of the wing. He could hear swearing coming from the car Agnes was in. A woman dragged herself out of the driver's seat. She was fat and moved slowly. The man who had sat next to Agnes on the back seat got out. They were quickly surrounded by a crowd of people.
Some of them wanted to help. The owner of one of the crashed cars was complaining loudly. Someone was calling for an ambulance. A woman was screaming in the third car. She was stuck in the wreckage. A young boy was standing in front of the car crying continually "Mummy, mummy!"

Übung 30: Welche Wörter gehören zusammen?

1. sound
a) ☐ spin b) ☐ whirr c) ☐ bounce

ÜBUNG 30 !

2. driving

a) ☐ overtake b) ☐ crouch c) ☐ burst

3. car

a) ☐ crowd b) ☐ stretcher c) ☐ tyre

4. road

a) ☐ handle b) ☐ seat c) ☐ lane

Sirens could be heard in the distance. Someone must have phoned the police and rescue services. The commotion was increasing. Hunter pushed his way through the people. He had to get Agnes out. But the fat woman did everything to stop him. She stood in his way and started hitting him. Hunter knocked her off her feet with a karate kick. She fell and rolled around on the floor. As Hunter approached her, someone punched him from behind. The pain shot through him. He fell to his knees. Some of the people nearby had seen what had happened. Chaos broke out for a moment. Then people turned their attention to the woman who was trapped in her car and watched as the fire-fighters started to cut the screaming woman out of the wreckage.

ÜBUNG 31 !

Übung 31: Bilden Sie aus dem Substantiv ein Adjektiv!

1. comfort ____________
2. nerve ____________
3. sympathy ____________
4. peace ____________
5. suspicion ____________
6. success ____________

Hunter struggled to his feet. In front of him stood the man from the back seat. The agent moved into position and felt for his pistol. It must have fallen out when he fell. "Then it's unarmed combat," he decided. His fist moved towards his opponent's face.
A sharp pain shot through his shoulder. The pain hit again when the woman pulled the knife out of the wound. He turned round as quick as a flash. A kick forced the fat woman to fall back onto the ground. She groaned as her head hit the hard concrete.
Her accomplice now pressed the barrel of his gun against Hunter's head. The agent took a deep breath. The next movement had to be perfect. He tensed his leg muscles.
But suddenly the pressure from the gun disappeared and he heard the man collapse. Hunter turned round.
Agnes was standing over the body of the man. She had an empty syringe in her raised hand. She was staring at the limp body at her feet.

Übung 32: Finden Sie die deutschen Entsprechungen für die englischen Idiome!

1. have a hunch	☐	ins Fettnäpfchen treten
2. get something off one's chest	☐	ein Geschick für etwas haben
3. make a fool of oneself	☐	jemanden von der kurzen Leine lassen
4. get on someone's nerves	☐	jemandem die Hölle heiß machen
5. have a knack for something	☐	sich lächerlich machen
6. put one's foot in it	☐	einen Verdacht haben
7. let someone off the leash	☐	jemandem auf die Nerven gehen
8. breathe down someone's neck	☐	sich etwas von der Seele reden

“Let’s go!” Hunter shouted to her. She lowered the syringe but did not move.
“Quick!” urged the agent. Finally she started to follow him. They ran back along the side of the road towards the city. After a while they stopped. They could hardly hear any noise from the accident anymore. Only “Mummy, mummy!” from time to time.

Agnes’s performance that morning gave Hunter hope. The idea of using the knock-out serum in the syringe was great. She must have brought a whole laboratory with her in her rucksack. Unfortunately the man was still in a coma and so they could not question him. He wondered whether he should do the break-in with Agnes after all. These people who continually attacked him were slowly getting on his nerves. But the afternoon of training would show that the biologist still had a few things to learn.

Agnes hit hardly any of the targets in shooting practice, neither with a pistol nor with the big machine gun. He broke off the climbing exercise after the first attempt. If she could not climb to the top, she certainly could not abseil in the training room. So there was no reason to try.
Training in the special operations suit was also unsuccessful. Agnes took too long in the ladies’ changing rooms just to get into the tight overall and put all the equipment in the right pockets. Hunter told her how to do it through the open door of the changing rooms.

ÜBUNG 33 !

Übung 33: Ordnen Sie die Buchstaben zu sinnvollen Wörtern!

1. TCKATA (Angriff) ______________________

2. CPTAIRCE (Übung) ______________________

3. RGTEAT (Ziel) ______________________

4. GEYSNIR (Spritze) ______________________

5. TEPTAMT (Versuch) ______________________

6. TCPOKE (Hosentasche) ______________________

7. LCIBM (klettern) ______________________

More than ever he regretted that there were not more female agents. Jenny Smith only arrived for training after three quarters of an hour. She at least helped Agnes put on her overall, but then had to go because her karate partner was waiting for her.

The break-in would be a fiasco. Callaghan was breathing down his neck because of the car crash. Paris and Berlin were reporting more deaths. The London Public Health Department had warned the public. But because they did not really know what they should warn people about, the announcement in the morning newspapers made people panic. The Public Health Department and other official offices were receiving lots of telephone calls.

"All I've got is a hunch and a security firm which is trying to kill me," thought Hunter with resignation. His shoulder hurt under the bandage. "Oh, and I've also got a hole in my shoulder thanks to the fat woman!"

Early the next morning Agnes reported to Kim Lee, the karate and martial arts trainer. It was his job to get her fighting fit. Hunter had other things to worry about.
He needed to study the plan of the "Mealomeal" building and think through the break-in the next day carefully.

Übung 34: Trifft die Aussage zu? Markieren Sie! Richtig ✔ oder falsch –?

ÜBUNG 34

1. There are lots of women agents in the Secret Service. ☐
2. Hunter practised karate with Agnes. ☐
3. The public now knew about the problem. ☐
4. People were not worried about the situation. ☐
5. Hunter wanted to break into Mealomeal with Agnes. ☐
6. Hunter had an injured shoulder. ☐

On his desk there were two letters waiting for him. One was a card from Percy, this time with a photo of countryside on it. Green hills and a glowing red sunset, and underneath in pink letters "Holidays in Kent". Hunter put the card away – he would read it later.

The letter was much more interesting to him. It came from the secret service communications centre. The thick envelope contained print-outs of emails from the secret services in other European countries. Attached to the front was a piece of paper which summarised what they had found out. Hunter skimmed through it. The symptoms were, as Callaghan had reported, the same, or at least very similar, in most cases. The time of death – midday or in the evening – was also the same in the majority of cases. Many of the authorities on the Continent suspected an allergic reaction. Some of the other suspicions were also listed – contaminated food additives, international terrorism, or someone blackmailing the company which produced ready-meals by threatening to poison their products.

None of them seemed any more believable than the original idea that it was a killer allergy.

Übung 35: Bilden Sie sinnvolle Sätze!

1. desk his Hunter a postcard on found.

---

2. report him the more gave information.

---

3. allergic could it been have reaction an.

---

4. really come knew from no one it where had.

---

5. any believe Hunter really the of didn't possibilities.

He leafed through to the back of the papers and looked for any other clues which the writers of the list might have overlooked or not found important.
He suddenly stopped when he read the reports from the French. They had suspected an international terrorist attack. They were not sure if it was just poison that had killed the people. Perhaps it was also a highly sophisticated biological weapons system?
In any case, there were no clues from the bodies about what might have caused death.
"So it's exactly like our pathologists – we're all groping in the dark!" mumbled Hunter.
Someone appeared from nowhere beside him. His head shot round. His eyes fell on a sharp piece of glass that was right beside his neck. He pushed his chair back quickly to get away from the glass.

He jumped out of his seat and knocked over the chair with a bang. Agnes was standing next to his desk, holding a little piece of glass and looking at the agent, shocked. Hunter ran his hand through his slightly wavy hair in confusion. He snapped at her, "What the hell are you doing? Are you trying out some new martial art you've just learnt?"

She looked at him in surprise. The shoulders in her baggy pullover shook a little.

"Then I won't tell you. I'll go."

"Hold on," he said quickly to calm her down. He had gone too far. "What is it?"

The girl chewed her bottom lip. But she soon stopped sulking.

"I think I have it. In the "Mealomeal" products there seems to be a large amount of genetically-modified food. That's normal in many substances these days."

She then told him about genetically-modified soya in chocolate bars and about the solution to the problem of hunger in the world through the development of high-yield, resistant types of cereals, vegetables and fruit. Hunter almost lost the thread. She talked about all kinds of substances and often used their chemical abbreviations or Latin names.

ÜBUNG 36 !

Übung 36: Setzen Sie die richtige Präposition ein!

1. He knocked ________ his coffee and burnt his hand.

2. It was so cold he put ________ his warmest pullover.

3. Could you switch ________ the TV – I'm trying to work.

4. The man in black got ________ of the car and fired his gun.

5. Quick, get ________! This is the bus stop we want.

6. He took ________ his key and unlocked the door.

Hunter did not dare to ask any questions. Secretly he had to admit that the girl knew what she was talking about. She then started to wave the piece of glass under his nose.

"And this could be the key to everything!" she ended triumphantly.

The agent looked at her hesitantly.

"And what might the key be?" he asked.

"Biological weapons which break down when they react with the body. No trace left for the autopsy."

Hunter was silent. Then he began: "Hmm. And what does that have to do with genetically-modified macaroni cheese?"

Agnes stopped looking like she knew everything. "Good question," she admitted. "I've got a substance from the blood of one of the bodies on this slide. It shows traces of "Tertechs". It was a biological weapon developed during the Cold War. Normally "Tertechs" doesn't leave any traces behind in the body. Unless it comes into contact with a particular substance which doesn't occur in nature during the reaction."

Hunter could not understand a word, but he didn't want to admit his ignorance to Agnes.

"I'll show you under the microscope!" the young woman announced. The agent was not convinced that that would help. But he had in the meantime understood that the little piece of glass was a slide. One of those pieces of glass you put under a microscope to test substances.

ÜBUNG 37 !

Übung 37: Enträtseln Sie die zwei zusammengehörenden Lösungswörter!

1. Spur ☐ _ _ _ _
2. Fertiggericht _ ☐ _ _ _ - _ _ _ _
3. überrascht _ _ _ _ _ _ ☐ _ _
4. Frage _ _ _ _ ☐ _ _ _
5. genetisch _ _ _ _ ☐ _ _
6. Pistole _ ☐ _
7. Abkürzung _ _ ☐ _ _ _ _ _ _ _ _ _
8. Fall _ _ _ ☐

Lösung: _ _ _ _ _ _ _ _

The motorway to Birmingham was empty and they arrived early. Hunter took the turn-off before the city. Soon afterwards he turned into the side road that led to Mealomeal.

The moon shone on the concrete of the road. After a few hundred metres the road became a gravel slope.

ÜBUNG 38 !

Übung 38: Lesen Sie weiter und unterstreichen Sie die englische Übersetzung folgender Wörter!

(1. verstecken, 2. Dunkelheit, 3. ganz, 4. Stacheldraht, 5. entdeckt, 6. Kombiauto, 7. Werkzeuge, 8. ungeschickt)

The agent did not like the bright moonlight much. The open fields beside the road which led to the company building offered nowhere to hide. They did not even have the cover of darkness.

Agnes had been silent for the whole journey. Hunter had not spoken, either. He had preferred to concentrate on what they had to do. He parked the car a short distance away from the barbed wire fence which he could see in front of them in the light of the searchlight. Would the car be discovered? It was worth a try. He loved his old estate car and did not want the same to happen to it as with Tina's Fiat.

Hunter jumped up and down in his special operations suit and waved his arms about in the air. He was warming up. The night was cold. Agnes was taking forever to get ready. She had already put on her suit when Hunter had picked her up from home. She was now taking all the other tools out of her shoulder bag. She was packing them clumsily into the pockets of her suit. She was finally ready.

The central locking engaged. Hunter spent a couple of seconds setting up a battery-operated electroshocker on the car door handle. "Just in case someone tries to touch my car!" he growled.

Übung 39: Bilden Sie aus dem Adjektiv ein Adverb!

ÜBUNG 39 !

1. slow ______________

2. strange ______________

3. bright ______________

4. unusual ______________

5. fast ______________

6. careful ______________

7. early ______________

The two agents set off. Hunter went in front. They jogged along the path towards the company building. They stayed close to the side of the road. They did not need a torch or night-vision glasses. The moon was still shining brightly.

They did not meet any cars. Their steps on the gravel crunched strangely in the night silence. They reached the barbed wire fence. Hunter tested the fence using an electricity detector which was built into his suit under his right arm.

The digital display of the tiny device showed nothing. Hunter took out a pair of metal cutters from his belt and cut through the wire. He made a hole.

"You go first," he whispered to Agnes. It took a while for her to get through clumsily. Hunter rolled his eyes.

Behind the fence they carried on. They ran faster. A three-metre high wall enclosed the company site. They sprinted the last part. Agnes overtook Hunter and stood hesitantly by the wall. Hunter came up behind her and pressed her against the wall.

! ÜBUNG 40

Übung 40: Beantworten Sie die Fragen zum Text!

1. How did Hunter and Agnes reach the company building?

2. How did Hunter test the barbed wire fence?

3. Was the fence electrified?

4. How did they get through the barbed wire fence?

5. Did Agnes find it easy to get through the fence?

6. What did they find all around the company site?

"You can't just walk around in the moonlight!" he hissed between his teeth. She did not answer.

Hunter moved along the cold stone wall. There was an iron gate a short distance away. He quickly checked that the metal was not electrified.

There was a little porter's office directly behind the gate and a small wooden hut with a large window at a right angle to the gate. Hunter pressed himself along the wall until he reached the bars of the gate. He looked all around carefully to check for cameras, but he could not see any.

He slowly went forward to risk a look in the hut. There was no one there. All he could see was a high table and behind it a wall with lots of television screens. He studied the black and white pictures on the monitors. Some of them showed factory halls with conveyor belts. Others showed offices and corridors. There were three pictures of laboratories. There were no people in any of the pictures.

He went a little further. He wanted to remember the pictures of the laboratories especially. That was exactly where he wanted to go. A figure appeared on one of the screens. It moved slowly and carefully. Hunter looked around. Then he looked back at the screen. He stepped back into the shadows, startled. The figure was him.

Übung 41: Übersetzen Sie folgende Sätze!

1. Er überprüfte, ob der Zaun sicher war.

2. Das Gitter war verschlossen.

3. Sie hatten vor, in das Firmengebäude einzubrechen.

4. Hunter ist ohne Mühe über die Mauer gesprungen.

5. Das helle Mondlicht war gefährlich für die Mission.

"Well?" said Agnes. She had crept up to him near the gate.
"Wait behind there," he hissed rudely.
"OK, I'll go back then," she replied. Since she had found traces of "Tertechs" which the other European secret services had not found, she had become much more self-confident. Hunter wondered if he should tell her that the French had also had similar suspicions. He decided against it. She would probably need a little self-confidence tonight.
The agent looked on the ground for a stone. When he had found a good one, he threw it over the wall. A dog started barking. A door opened a short way off. The barking only stopped after a man's voice spoke to the dog to calm it down. Steps approached the gate.
"Who's there?" came a shout from inside the yard.
Hunter and Agnes pressed themselves against the wall. The agent

felt the cold of the stones through his suit. “Thermal suits!” he thought bitterly. He then concentrated on breathing as quietly as possible. Next to him, Agnes was hardly breathing at all. She took a breath from time to time, then held it as long as she could. Then she breathed in again carefully through her nose.
The beam of a torch shone through the gate. The light moved left, then into the middle, then right.
“No one there, Rover,” the guard said to the dog. Hunter could hear the dog panting. Otherwise everything was silent.

Übung 42: Welches Wort hat eine ähnliche Bedeutung?

ÜBUNG 42 !

1. rude
   a) ☐ noisy
   b) ☐ impolite
   c) ☐ quick

2. pant
   a) ☐ choke
   b) ☐ breathe
   c) ☐ run

3. calm
   a) ☐ pleasant
   b) ☐ heavy
   c) ☐ relaxed

There was a crackle, followed by a static hiss. A voice spoke from a radio.
“What’s wrong?”

"There's no one here," said the guard behind the gate loudly.
There was another hiss and then: "Come back in, man. It's your turn!"
"Strip poker without any women is stupid!" Hunter heard.
"Then bring another man and we'll play bridge!"
A final crackle ended the radio conversation. The beam of light from the torch jumped about on the ground. The man disappeared. Agnes and Hunter looked at each other.
"The security firm again," thought Hunter. He was really sick of them.
The camera pictures showed that there was no one working in the factory at that time. The conveyor belts stood still. So the only way of getting caught was the security guards.
"I mean, the card players," the agent corrected himself. He gave Agnes a sign with his hand to follow him. They moved to the point where the gate was. There they stopped until they heard the door close. The guard was back inside the building. To be sure, Hunter waited a few moments. Remembering where the cameras were, he crept forward. He checked the TV screens to make sure he could not be seen on the monitors. He signalled to the biologist to stay directly behind him.

ÜBUNG 43 !

Übung 43: Welches Wort ist gemeint?

1. The light from a torch.

____

2. The part of a television where the picture is.

____

3. The place where a company makes its products.

---

4. To speak very quietly.

---

5. The place where scientists do experiments.

She followed him like a shadow. The agent jumped up powerfully. He got hold of the top of the gate. He pulled himself up, climbed over the gate and jumped down into the yard. He landed almost silently.

Agnes tried to do the same. She fell back down onto the ground a couple of times. Her last jump was good enough. She reached the top of the gate. But she was not strong enough to climb up.

The agent groaned inside. Should he look for the way to open the gate in the porter's office? Too dangerous. So he jumped up, climbed back over the gate and was next to her again. She no longer had any self-confidence.

Hunter put his hands together to make a kind of platform for her. She had to try a couple of times before she managed to climb over the fence. Her shoes made a loud noise when she landed on the other side.

Hunter quickly followed. He grabbed her arm and pulled her to the wall behind the hut.

It was quiet. No one had heard the noise from her shoes. Hunter wanted to tell her off, but decide not to. They had no time to lose. They had to get into the building.

ÜBUNG 44 !

Übung 44: Unterstreichen Sie die richtige Alternative!

1. They had no time to loose/lose
2. The sun was very hot, so they sat in the shadow/shade.
3. The gangsters weren't very sympathetic/nice.
4. The factory was very great/big.
5. Hunter's actual/current mission was very dangerous.
6. Some people are more sensible/sensitive to food allergies than others.
7. The salary/loan for being a secret agent wasn't very good.

They crept along the wall and followed it around the yard. The few lights in the yard hardly gave any light. But in the moonlight they found the way with no problems. They reached the flat building which stretched out in front of them. There was still no one around. Hunter saw the plan of the complex in his head. He counted the steps. The rubber soles of his shoes made hardly any noise on the ground in the yard. He passed two big doors. He stopped at a small metal door. This had to be the door. It was a side entrance which led directly into the staircase.

Hunter wanted to open the door with one of the lockpicks on his belt. But there was no lock. He took off his blue rucksack and unzipped the side pocket. He took out a hand-sized welding torch. He turn it on to full power. He put it on the metal around the door handle. He carefully moved the jet around it.

Quick footsteps approached. A muffled whistle could be heard. Then a dull thud. The agent turned around quickly. The welding torch was still on. Agnes had to jump out of the way.

She then shrugged her shoulders and looked at the ground a little surprised. A man in a thick black jacket was lying there. She had put him to sleep for the next ten hours with her stun gun.

"This time not the syringe, but a real agent's weapon," thought Hunter. He had to admire her quick reaction.

Übung 45: Bilden Sie die Gegenteile mit dem richtigen Präfix!
(ir-, im-, in-, un-)

ÜBUNG 45 !

1. zip ______________________
2. relevant ______________________
3. pleasant ______________________
4. probable ______________________
5. direct ______________________
6. fortunate ______________________
7. responsible ______________________

The biologist was still holding the pistol in her hand. She nodded to Hunter to continue. He carried on cutting. A few seconds later he took the whole lock out of the door and put it on the ground. When he had put the welding torch in his rucksack, he looked around at Agnes.

She was kneeling on the ground next to the guard searching his pockets. Hunter hurried over to her, pulled her up and dragged her out of the beam coming from the yard light. He quickly placed her next to the wall and ran over to the guard. He grabbed his legs and pulled his limp and heavy body into the shadow. He hoped that the other guards had not seen anything.

Perhaps there were other places where you could see the camera pictures, not only in the porter's office?

He left the unconscious man lying by the wall and took Agnes's hand.

"No radio or anything," she said in a quiet voice. Hunter said nothing. They entered the building together.

Übung 46: Setzen Sie die richtige Form des Simple Past ein!

The staircase (1. to be) __________ narrow. There (2. to be) __________ not many lights. The grey walls must have been white at one time. Thick cobwebs (3. to cover) __________ the corners. Hunter (4. to know) __________ the plan:

"The emergency exit," he (5. to whisper) __________. He (6. to turn) __________ to Agnes. She was standing on the landing that (7. to go) __________ downstairs. She was drawing shapes in the dust with her boots. As he (8. to come) __________ nearer, he (9. to see) __________ she had made little flowers from footprints that were there. He pulled the biologist to one side and (10. to kneel) __________ down.

"Boots, big boots without a heel. About size 45." The lights on the ceiling only gave out a very dull light. Agnes switched on her torch and shone it onto the floor. There were other footprints, small ones, too. Some of them went down to the cellar, others went upstairs. Hunter looked at the woman, amazed. The light from the torch shone in his eyes and blinded him.

"What did you think you were doing?" he hissed angrily.

"My goodness!" she said. Shocked, she added: "Sorry."

They crept along the wall down into the cellar. It was the fastest way to find the laboratories.

"Three labs, with a camera in each," said Hunter. "Plus a camera right at the back in the corridor – or was it at the front?" He crouched on the last step. He studied the ceiling.

The beam from the torch found a camera in the opposite corner of the ceiling.

"Switch it off!" cried Hunter again in a panicked voice. The torch went out. He took his night vision glasses out of his belt. Would they follow the light from Agnes's torch and catch them easily?

Übung 47: Wie heißt das Wort auf Englisch?

ÜBUNG 47 !

1. Decke	☐ dust
2. Keller	☐ welding torch
3. gegenüber	☐ heel
4. kriechen	☐ cobweb
5. blenden	☐ ceiling
6. Staub	☐ opposite
7. Spinnengewebe	☐ crawl
8. Schuhabsatz	☐ buzz
9. Schweißbrenner	☐ cellar
10. summen	☐ blind

"Put your night vision glasses on. Get rid of the torch," he ordered. While he was stretching to get under the camera, Agnes listened behind her. She tried to find her glasses noisily.

When he pulled the cable out of the camera, something clattered behind him. The biologist had dropped her glasses. Luckily they were made of an unbreakable material.

They crept along the corridor, which looked green through the glasses. There were signs on the doors. Hunter stopped in front of "Laboratory 1 – Development". There was a combination lock on the wall beside the door. He connected his codebreaker and watched the red numbers which appeared and disappeared on the display of the tiny metal box. There was a buzz and the door unlocked. He put the gadget back in his suit pocket and pushed open the door. He signalled to Agnes to wait outside. First he wanted to find the camera.

Earlier, in the porter's office, he had wondered if he should start a picture loop. Then the cameras would show a freeze frame and he would not have to look for each one and switch it off. Switching off was always dangerous. One of the guards might decide to do some repairs at night and burst in on the operation.

With these guards, he decided he could do it. They did not seem to be trained professionals. He hated "card players". He broke the picture transmission easily by cutting through the cable. The room had a low ceiling. He only had to stretch out his arm with the metal cutters to cut through the wire. He put the cutters back in his belt.

Against his instructions, Agnes had entered the room. She had already put her rucksack on the laboratory table and was unpacking all her test equipment. She had thought of everything.

"Bring me the stuff to analyse," she whispered.

That was not so easy. Where should he look? He went to a wooden cabinet.

"Not there!" Agnes called out in a whisper. "Only metal cabinets. Samples of liquids are always in metal cabinets."

Hunter felt like a schoolboy.

"I'll do it," she continued. "Check the other two labs and look for …" What exactly he should look for she did not say.

Übung 48: Beantworten Sie die Fragen zum Text!

1. Why did Hunter order Agnes to switch off her torch?

2. Why didn't Agnes's glasses smash when she dropped them?

3. How did Hunter open the door to Laboratory 1?

4. Why did Hunter order Agnes to stay outside Laboratory 1?

5. How did Hunter switch off the camera?

Hunter returned to the corridor. No sign of the guards. He looked briefly in the staircase, where the dull emergency lighting shone. The corridor he was walking down was unlit. he read the sign on the next door with his night vision glasses: "Kitchen". As he passed he thought of Percy, who always made tea for him in the office. He thought of Kent.
He paused. "Where do you hide illegal stuff? Where no one will look for it, so somewhere that is obvious." He immediately went back to the kitchen. It was locked. He broke open the door with a lockpick and went in.
A table and two chairs, a sink and a coffee machine, and a small cooker with two hot plates.

ÜBUNG 49

Übung 49: Unterstreichen Sie das „schwarze Schaf“!

1. knife, cupboard, shelf, armchair
2. crowd, group, loner, team
3. obvious, necessary, clear, evident
4. plane, truck, estate car, jeep
5. cauliflower, pea, pineapple, cucumber
6. finger, throat, nail thumb
7. creep, dash, run, hurry

"Where do you keep samples?" he repeated in his head. He open the small fridge. The door hit against something. Hunter looked at the floor. There was a body hidden halfway under the table. The figure groaned quietly. The agent squatted down. It was a man. His legs were tied up. His arms were tied behind his back with rope. When Hunter touched the body, the man groaned. Hunter pulled him out from under the table. His face was very thin and his eyes were bloodshot. There was a towel tied around his mouth. The agent loosened it.

"Please, don't hit me," begged the man in a broken voice. "Let me go."

"Who are you?" asked Hunter. The man looked at him shocked.

"Stop, please stop. Let me go."

"Who are you?" repeated the agent.

"No more games, please. You can have everything. Take the company. Do what you want with it. Make things, deliver things, but please let me go."

Hunter shook the man. "Wake up, man!"

As he untied the rope, he asked him again: "I'll get you out of here, but tell me who you are."

The man rolled onto his front so that Hunter could untie the rope.

"Wayne Carter, director. I'm the director of "Mealomeal". Or I should better say I was."
"Carry on," said Hunter impatiently and started untying the man's feet.
"Who are you?" asked the man suddenly.
"A friend," answered Hunter. Then he decided to tell the truth. "OK. British Secret Service."

Übung 50: Wie lauten die Sätze in der richtigen Reihenfolge?

ÜBUNG 50 !

1. under man Hunter the found table the.

2. untied he rope hands his around the.

3. hurt anymore please me don't.

4. asked the what he doing there was man.

5. man agent told was he the an he.

"Secret service?" whimpered Carter. "I had nothing to do with it," he began quickly. "I just wanted to make my frozen food. If someone can help a bit, that's not a bad thing, is it? As long as it tastes good." Hunter had to swallow. "I only paid for the development of genetically improved seeds. I know it's illegal. But Turner told me everyone was doing it."

Hunter helped the man to sit up. His face was twisted with pain as he continued: "Out there, the fields. That's all supposed to be land for growing vegetables and cereals. Turner's people played around with the best seeds in my labs. And then all this."
Hunter stopped him. They had no time to lose.
"Where's the hot material?"
The director was not listening. "I'm just the owner of a medium-sized business, the competition is big. I told Turner that I didn't want that. I don't care if there's money to be made with deliveries like that. I want to be honest. Just a bit of genetic manipulation. That's not dishonest, everyone's doing it."
"Where the deadly stuff?" Hunter shook the man again. His grey hair was dirty. His cheeks were unshaved. Hunter took out an energy bar from his boot leg and gave it to the man. He bit into it as if he had not eaten for weeks.
After three bites the bar was finished. "I think in Lab 1. In the other two they really developed seeds. I was never allowed to go into the front one. We'll never get in because there's a combination lock on the door."

! ÜBUNG 51

Übung 51: Finden Sie ein Synonym für die Wörter in Klammern!

1. Hunter unlocked the door (quickly) ______________________

2. Hunter (said again) __________________ that he was an agent.

3. Carter was very (slim) ______________________

4. He (dragged) ________________ the man from under the table.

5. Carter wanted to be (truthful) ______________________

Hunter held the director by the arm and dragged him behind. The man stumbled a couple of times. The agent only then realised that the man was not wearing any night vision glasses. Everything must have been dark and shadowy.
"My name's Hunter," he said on the way through the lab door. "This is my colleague Westcombe," he added and pointed at Agnes. She turned round.
"That's it," she said happily and nodded at a test tube with yellow liquid in it.
There was a noise from the stairs.
"Oh no!" said Carter.
"Under the table!" Hunter ordered and pushed the man forward. He himself ducked behind the wooden cabinet on the wall.
Agnes stood defencelessly in the middle of the room, holding the test tube. Hunter signalled to her to hide, but she stared petrified at the door.

Übung 52: Was gehört zusammen? Kreuzen Sie an!

ÜBUNG 52 !

1. TV	☐ food
2. test	☐ table
3. open-plan	☐ screen
4. toilet	☐ lock
5. kitchen	☐ machine
6. frozen	☐ seat
7. coffee	☐ office
8. combination	☐ tube

Two figures passed by.
"Switching off the cameras! If this is one of Mike's tricks, I'll be really annoyed. Where on earth is he?" said one of them.

"He's probably asleep somewhere. Whose turn is it to give the prisoner something to eat?"
"Yours!" the other one answered.
"Just my luck!" said his colleague. "Hey, the door …" Suddenly both of them were silent. They entered the room and one of them switched on the light on the wall. The room filled with bright light. Agnes was still standing there.
"Are you still working?" asked the bigger of the two men. His partner nudged him in the ribs. He then noticed that she was not wearing a lab coat but some kind of fighting suit.
"Tell Turner," shouted the smaller man loudly and took out his gun and aimed it at the woman.
Agnes continued to hold the test tube without saying a word. The man opposite her waited until his partner had finished his conversation with Turner. As he put the mobile phone away, he mumbled: "The boss was angry. He was already in bed. But he'll be here soon."
"Now to you, darling," said the other one. He waved his pistol threateningly in front of her nose. She had pushed her night vision glasses onto her forehead. Her eyes turned towards the yellow liquid in the test tube. The two guards followed her eyes. Should she explain to them that it's probably "Tertechs"? A biological weapon which leads to a quick death if it is eaten or it enters the blood?

! ÜBUNG 53

Übung 53: Enträtseln Sie das Lösungswort!

1. Sicherheit □ _ _ _ _ _
2. geheim _ _ _ _ _ □
3. atmen _ _ _ □ _ _ _

4. flüstern _ _ □ _ _ _ _

5. Wachmann _ _ _ □ _

6. Taschenlampe _ _ _ □ _

7. verschwinden _ _ _ □ _ _ _ _ _

8. Lärm _ _ _ □ _

9. Lichtstrahl _ □ _ _

Lösung: _ _ _ _ _ _ _ _ _

"This is acid," she lied. "Do you know what it's like to have the skin fall off your bones?"

The man lowered his gun, shocked. At that exact moment a stun dart from Hunter's pistol hit him. He dropped to the floor immediately. His colleague fired at the wooden cabinet. He missed the agent because he ducked, but it was close. The guard spun round and fired at Agnes, who was trying to take out her gun with her one free hand.

She had no cover. She screamed loudly as the bullet hit her arm and fell to her knees. Like an executioner, the gunman walked towards her. He placed the end of his gun carefully on her forehead.

"Come out, or the little one here is dead," he shouted towards the cabinet. Hunter threw his pistol into the room. It slid over the floor and stopped directly at the man's feet. Hunter came out from behind the cabinet with his hands up. He looked worriedly at Agnes, then looked directly at the man. The man looked him straight in the eyes and said:

"Get down here next to your friend." Hunter walked slowly to Agnes, who was groaning quietly on the floor. His eyes never left the attacker.

Übung 54: Welche Wörter gehören zusammen?

1. slide
a) ☐ smash b) ☐ slow c) ☐ slip

2. groan
a) ☐ moan b) ☐ creep c) ☐ bend

3. spin
a) ☐ hurry b) ☐ turn c) ☐ leap

4. elbow
a) ☐ head b) ☐ leg c) ☐ arm

A tinkling noise came from under the table. The guard turned. Agnes used this second to ram her uninjured elbow hard into the man's stomach. He shouted and started shooting. The bullets hit the floor. Hunter pushed Agnes quickly under the table. Before he could stand up again, he felt the man's gun in his back.
"Don't move an inch!" he snarled at Hunter. He was already part way under the table. The man had to bend down to aim the gun at the agent. A heavy boot hit his hand from the side. Agnes kicked him again. She had rolled under the table to one side to make room for Hunter and was now at a right angle to the attacker. He screamed and dropped his gun. Hunter kicked out behind him. His foot hit the man full in the face. His nose split open. The man put both his hands to his nose and howled.
Hunter crawled out from under the table as quick as a flash. He picked up his stun gun and fired at the man. The man groaned briefly then fell to the floor.

Übung 55: Ordnen Sie die Buchstaben zu sinnvollen Wörtern!

"Agnes, are you OK?" 1. eksad __________ (fragte) the agent, worried.

Instead of her voice, he heard the director say, "Watch out! There are bits of glass from the test tube everywhere. Be 2. lcfraeu __________ (vorsichtig)!"

Her head appeared from under the table. Hunter jumped over to help her. The director also crawled out and had the 3. misrane __________ (Reste) of a test tube in his hand.

"I just wanted to create a diversion," he apologised, and looked at the 4. icepse __________ (Stücke) of glass.

The sound of 5. ptosfeots __________ (Schritte) could be heard on the stairs. Hunter pushed Agnes back under the table. He took two cardboard 6. sobxe __________ (Kisten) from near the wall and put them in front of her for protection. It had to be good 7. ohenug __________ (genug) for the moment.

"Come quickly!" he called to the director and signalled to him to hide behind the 8. tibncea __________ (Schrank). Carter did not follow him, but just sat on the table.

"What's going on here?" growled Turner as he entered the laboratory. He was about 1.70 metres tall and stocky. It really did seem that the phone call had got him out of bed. He was only wearing jeans and a faded T-shirt under his open winter coat. He looked from the two guards on the floor to Carter.

"I see," said Turner. His movements became slower. He moved towards the director and took his gun out of his coat pocket.

ÜBUNG 56 !

Übung 56: Haben die Wörter eine ähnliche Bedeutung? Markieren Sie! Richtig ✔ oder falsch – ?

1. faded/colourful ☐
2. shoot/fire ☐
3. prison/jail ☐
4. calm/annoyed ☐
5. properly/correctly ☐
6. fool/idiot ☐

"You can't frighten me with that," the director said calmly. Turner stood still for a moment. Carter continued. "You've taken everything from me – my company, my ideals, my dreams. Mealomeal is dead because of your madness."

Turner laughed. "You poor little man. I gave you the chance many times. You could have worked with us. We produce a few genetically-modified seeds for you, and you supply your ready-meal factory from your own field. We would have made the firm a success."

Carter looked at the bodies on the floor. He looked back at Turner. "I wanted to make food products. I didn't want to kill anyone because someone put a weapons delivery in a pallet for the supermarket by mistake."

Turner moved impatiently towards him. He placed the barrel of his gun on his chest. "You idiot! I thought you would have become a bit cleverer in your kitchen prison. But if you haven't …"

A hiss broke the silence. Hunter's shot had missed Turner by an inch. He could not aim properly from his position behind the cabinet. Turner spun around from Carter and fired at the cabinet. Behind it, Hunter was trying to reload his gun. The box with the stun darts in his belt was empty. He had more in his rucksack on the floor, but that would take too long.

He pulled his other loaded gun out of his left boot. It was hardly bigger than his hand, but it was deadly. And he wanted Turner alive!

Übung 57: Welche Übersetzung ist richtig?

1. Warum wolltest du das machen?
   - a) ☐ Why did you do that?
   - b) ☐ Why did you want to do that?
   - c) ☐ Why did you that?

2. Hunter versuchte gerade, seine Pistole zu finden.
   - a) ☐ Hunter was trying to find his gun.
   - b) ☐ Hunter tried to find his gun.
   - c) ☐ Hunter had tried to find his gun.

3. Er gab ihr das Reagenzglas zurück.
   - a) ☐ He gave to her back the test tube.
   - b) ☐ He gave her back the test tube.
   - c) ☐ He gave back her the test tube.

Hunter jumped expertly from his cover and aimed at the man. Turner fired a shot in Hunter's direction. Hunter jumped out of the way, slid along the floor and rolled to the side. The bullet hit the wall in the exact place where he had stood. A frightening scream rang through the laboratory.

Carter stabbed again. Turner sank to the floor holding his arm. Blood spurted out of the wound. Carter stood behind him holding the piece of glass threateningly.

"Do you want some more?" he shouted. He was about to use the glass again when Hunter ordered him to stop.

"It's over!" he cried. Carter lowered the glass. He kicked Turner hard in the back. "Bastard!"

"Stop it, man!" A few men came through the door.

"At last!" groaned Turner. He stood up with difficulty and began to look more closely at his wound. It hurt terribly. He turned his anger on the guards.

"Can you tell me what took you so long? Kevin, take these three to the airport. I'll discuss the rest with Stan. I'll see you all early tomorrow morning. Then we talk about what "Alarm" means!"

Turner busied himself with his wound again. He swore loudly and left the laboratory.

ÜBUNG 58 !

Übung 58: Wie lautet das Verb im Simple Past?

1. slide ______________________
2. shoot ______________________
3. stand ______________________
4. become ______________________
5. hit ______________________
6. apologise ______________________
7. bend ______________________

The three prisoners could not escape. The rucksack with the other weapons was behind the cabinet. Agnes was hit and Carter did not think he could get them all out of there. He did not even have the piece of glass in his hand anymore.

Hunter gave up and let himself be taken by the muscular man called Kevin. Another one got the biologist from under the table. She looked at Hunter. He tried to look confident. He was not successful.

Carter was tied up. He seemed used to it. He stared silently at the floor and did not try to stop them. Hunter counted the men. There were eleven of them and Kevin. There really was no chance of escape at the moment.

The prisoners were taken up the stairs and outside. A delivery van was waiting in the yard. They were pushed along at gunpoint and loaded into the back of the van. Six of the guards got in with them. There was no chance of having a private conversation yet.

Übung 59: Ordnen Sie das Buchstabenchaos zu sinnvollen Wörtern!

ÜBUNG 59 !

1. MTORWORO (morgen) ______________________

2. ROSPEINR (Gefangener) ______________________

3. HEATNRET (drohen) ______________________

4. TDOSEUI (draußen) ______________________

5. TNIDORCIE (Richtung) ______________________

6. ENOCTECR (Asphalt) ______________________

7. CSAMER (Schrei) ______________________

The van left the company site through the gate. The people in the back were shaken around badly when the van accelerated. It bounced over the holes in the gravel road. Agnes sighed loudly once. Otherwise she was silent. Hunter had to admit that she was very brave. After all, there was still a bullet in her arm.

They drove past the estate car.

"Is that yours?" asked one of the men. He poked Hunter in the ribs with his gun.

"No, it's Father Christmas's!" he replied.

"Well, merry Christmas!" the guard laughed.

Another guard added, "And a happy New Year!"

After he said this, he pulled the pin out of a hand grenade on his belt. He held it in his hand and counted slowly. Hunter was not the only one to think he counted too slowly.

"Put that away, you idiot!" one of the other guards shouted. The guard laughed. The hand grenade flew through the air and landed a couple of metres in front of Hunter's car. A second later it exploded loudly. The agent looked at his dear car on fire. There was another blast, this time more powerful. The car flew into the air in a ball of flame. Pieces of metal fell from the sky. Hunter could not see any more. The van was too far away.

"Now I'm really angry!" he said to himself. "My poor car!"

! ÜBUNG 60

Übung 60: Markieren Sie! Richtig ✔ oder falsch –?

1. Hunter und Agnes saßen in einem LKW. ☐
2. Es war Weihnachten. ☐
3. Hunter hatte eine Handgranate dabei. ☐
4. Der Wachmann sprengte Hunters Auto in die Luft. ☐
5. Hunter war es egal, dass sein Auto kaputt war. ☐

The journey to the airport did not take long. It was terribly cold. As they were pushed down from the back of the van, the agent could hardly move his frozen legs. He looked at Agnes and saw that she was getting even worse. Carter, on the other hand, seemed to be in a trance. He did not speak. He did not moan. He just did what he was told.

Übung 61: Setzen Sie die richtige Präposition ein!

ÜBUNG 61

They were 1. ________________ the runway. Hunter's foot stood 2. _________ a hole 3. ________ the concrete where grass was growing. Clouds were now covering the moon. On one side he could see light shining 4. ________ some windows in the darkness. There must have been some kind 5. __________ hut there. A few other figures were approaching 6. __________ there.

"Good evening, Stan!" said Kevin 7. __________ the old man in a flying jacket who reached them first.

"Norman, bring the baby out," he answered. He looked 8. __________ the prisoners carefully in the van lights. Then he disappeared into the darkness again. To Hunter's right, the large doors of a hangar opened. Light streamed 9. ______________ of the building. A military plane rolled 10. ____________ slowly. That had to be the old man's "baby", Hunter realised. It was a small army transport plane.

When the plane was in position, two of Kevin's men went to the back of it. They pushed the prisoners inside the plane. The cargo door locked behind them with a bang. They were alone. Outside on the runway they could hear orders being shouted. There was a hectic hustle and bustle. Above them, they heard footsteps and shouts. Clearly Kevin's men were sitting in the passenger seats above the cargo hold.

The plane started moving. First slowly, then faster and faster. There was a short break because they stopped the plane again and checked the engines.

Übung 62: Finden Sie das passende Gegenteil!

1. difficult ______________________
2. heavy ______________________
3. decrease ______________________
4. arrive ______________________
5. early ______________________
6. top ______________________
7. safe ______________________

Hunter used the delay to take a few precautions. He searched blindly for something that they could hold onto during the take-off. They also needed blankets or something similar. It would get very cold as soon as they were in the air. Deadly cold.

The first thing his fingers touched was a wooden box, which was tied to the back part of the plane. He cut his hands as he tried to

open the top. Carter had woken up and came to help, but he could not do anything because his hands were still tied.
Hunter realised that not everyone was as good at untying themselves as he was. He untied Carter for the second time that night.
While the director was trying hard to open the box, Hunter went over quickly to Agnes.
She was lying still on the cold metal floor of the plane. He heard her breathing softly.
"Don't worry," he reassured her gently. "We'll get out of here and everything will be fine!"
"Stop talking, hero, and find us something to cover ourselves with and to hold onto during take-off," she complained.
"That's how I like you!" said Hunter. The woman always surprised him. She groaned a little, then lay still again. In the meantime, Carter had been successful. Hunter stumbled back to him in the dark. He felt inside the box. Some wood shavings and here and there a few sticks of dynamite and a few hand grenades.
"That'll keep us warm!" said the director happily, and began throwing out the wood shavings.
"Stop it!" shouted Hunter. "There are explosives packed in it. You'll kill us all!"
Carter stopped immediately. They carefully removed the wood shavings from the box. Hunter helped Agnes to lean on the side of the plane. He covered her with the wood shavings. Then he took some for himself. He sat next to her and supported her. Carter sat next to her on the other side.

Übung 63: Unterstreichen Sie die richtige Alternative!

ÜBUNG 63 !

The plane had started moving again. This time it accelerated faster. A gentle bounce told them that they had (1.) left/jumped the ground. Carter sat closest to the box. He had to try hard to support himself against it. The weight of the other two was pressing on him because the plane was climbing. He groaned, but supported them well.

Hunter's arm was around the biologist's shoulder. She had one hand around the place where the bullet had entered.

"Don't get any (2.) ideas/thoughts," she warned the agent. Shortly after she fell asleep.

The plane reached cruising altitude. Carter sighed with relief. The plane was (3.) now/actually horizontal in the air. He did not have to push against the box with all his strength.

"Do you have any idea where we are going?" he asked Hunter. "No. But let's (4.) save/spare our energy. Go to sleep," the agent answered.

The director did not feel like sleeping. Only after Hunter had explained to him how ice-cold it would become even with the wood shavings and that they should limit themselves to the simplest body movements did the director agree.

"All right. We'll take things easy. Let's not use any energy.“

When Carter had also fallen asleep, Hunter finally had a little peace and (5.) quiet/silence. For the moment he could not do (6.) anything/nothing.

ÜBUNG 64 !

Übung 64: Übersetzen Sie folgende Sätze!

1. Agnes ist schnell eingeschlafen.

---

2. Hunter löste zunächst das Seil.

---

3. Beeil dich!

---

4. Der Boden des Flugzeuges war sehr kalt.

---

5. Das Flugzeug startete langsam.

The plane landed roughly. The flight could not have been long. Hunter had the feeling that he had only slept for a couple of hours. The door to the cargo hold was opened. Several men in big boots marched in and dragged the three prisoners to their feet.

“What's that?” one of them asked when he saw the wood shavings everywhere.

“Just hurry up!” another shouted. Hunter recognised him. It was the one that Turner had called Kevin. Kevin told his companions to check the open ammunition box. He himself watched the prisoners, who were sitting on the floor. When he saw that they had untied themselves, he said angrily:

“What idiot tied them up? Anderson, Manning – you do it, and properly!”

The young men grabbed them roughly. First they tied up carter and Hunter, then the girl. Agnes whimpered a little as they put her arms behind her back. Then she gritted her teeth. She made no more sound. Hunter was again impressed by her bravery.

Anderson punched him in the back and pushed him forward. At first the agent wanted to fight back, but he thought it better not to. At the moment they had no chance against so many men.

A beautiful morning sun hit them. It was only now that the agent noticed how cold it had been inside the plane. He turned his face to the sky to let it warm up by the rays of the sun. Carter and Agnes did the same.

! ÜBUNG 65

Übung 65: Wie heißt das Wort auf Englisch? Ordnen Sie zu!

1. Flugzeug	☐ ammunition
2. packen	☐ forwards
3. Strahl	☐ hurry
4. Munition	☐ grab
5. vorwärts	☐ punch
6. Mut	☐ plane
7. sich beeilen	☐ notice
8. schlagen	☐ whimper
9. wimmern	☐ ray
10. merken	☐ bravery

They were on a runway which belonged to a dilapidated airport. The surface of the runway had deep potholes full of water and snow. The plane had stopped directly in front of the hangar. It was really more of a building than a hangar. An off-road vehicle was already waiting. Two men and a woman got out. Kevin greeted them.

"Dutch," the agent decided. So they were on the Continent. Kevin and his men hurried to hand over the prisoners. A few minutes later, Kevin and his men were again sitting in the same old plane, travelling back.

The butt of a gun hit Carter's shoulder with a crack. He fell weakly to his knees. The big guy who had hit him laughed. He shouted something in Dutch. Then he added in English:

"There's more where that came from – unless you're a good boy!"

The two men and the woman laughed. The other man was a little taller than Hunter. He held the agent in front of himself by his tied arms. The woman was thin and wiry. Her careworn face made her look hard. That seemed to match her character. She grabbed Agnes roughly to put her on the back seat of the off-road vehicle. To do this, her fingers held Agnes tightly on the exact place where the bullet had entered her arm.

Übung 66: Welches Substantiv wird beschrieben?

ÜBUNG 66 !

1. A person in jail.

2. The building where you keep planes.

3. The thing you fire from a gun.

4. The part of an airport where a plane lands.

5. The part of a gun you hold.

Hunter was placed next to Agnes. The third guy did not seem finished with Carter. He hit him again with the butt of his gun. The director, who was still on his knees, fell flat. His face landed in some snow. The man bent down towards him. He pushed his face into the dirty water with obvious enjoyment. Carter gasped for air as he pulled him out briefly.

"Stop messing around!" the woman shouted angrily. She had already taken her place in the driver's seat. She started the engine as her colleague dragged Carter up into the off-road vehicle and squashed him next to Agnes on the back seat.

He went and sat in the passenger seat.

Hunter glanced at Carter's dirty face. There was blood over one of his eyebrows. On the other side, Agnes slumped onto his shoulder. She had to be absolutely freezing in her black special operations suit. Hunter shivered. He was also cold after all that time.

ÜBUNG 67 !

Übung 67: Welche Wörter gehören zusammen?

1. plane
   a) ☐ windscreen
   b) ☐ passenger
   c) ☐ torch

2. prisoner
   a) ☐ handle
   b) ☐ mirror
   c) ☐ guard

3. cold
   a) ☐ cry
   b) ☐ leap
   c) ☐ shiver

The short journey took them from the small private airport to a wide motorway. After about half an hour they turned off this road. They drove through a suburb of Rotterdam. Finally, they turned into a side road. It led through harvested fields and greenhouses to a farm which stood on its own in a large open field. They stopped there.

The three prisoners were taken to the sheds next to the main building. They were locked up in a small room in one of the sheds, which was empty except for a few tools.

The tools must not have been used for years. Iron chains hung on the wall. There were brushes and the handle of a broken rake. The ground was covered in straw. When the woman and her two colleagues locked the door, it went dark inside. They heard a padlock being put on the door. Then the steps moved away outside the shed, which they locked as well.

Übung 68: Lesen Sie weiter und unterstreichen Sie die englische Übersetzung der folgenden Wörter!
(1. Seile, 2. Holzwände, 3. Wunde, 4. Stroh, 5. Riss, 6. Gürtel, 7. Betäubungsmittel, 8. Notfall)

ÜBUNG 68 !

Hunter first untied himself. One of the simplest things he had to do. These people did not seem to be complete professionals. They used ropes to tie up their victims. Any real gangster nowadays used plastic cords. No one could get out of those. But this …

He quickly freed Carter and Agnes. He placed her on a bed of straw. He inspected the wound in the little light which came through the gaps in the wooden walls. The bullet must not be allowed to stay in. They had taken his belt from him. He had a scalpel in it which was exactly what he needed. There was also anaesthetic so that he could carry out an emergency operation like this. He could not do it without all that.

Übung 69: Enträtseln Sie das Lösungswort!

1. zustimmen _ □ _ _ _
2. Kugel _ _ _ _ _ □ _
3. Wunde _ _ _ □ _
4. Schulter _ _ _ _ _ _ □ _
5. binden □ _ _
6. Kette _ _ _ □ _
7. entkommen _ _ □ _ _ _
8. Schuppen □ _ _ _

Lösung: _ _ _ _ _ _ _ _

"How can we help her?" asked Carter, worried.
"No idea," said Hunter.
"And it's all my fault," whimpered the director.
Before he could go on, the first lock was opened. Footsteps approached and the second lock was opened. Hunter and Carter quickly put their hands behind their backs so that it looked like they were still tied up.
The woman entered with a tray. She put three bowls onto the ground. There was a greeny-brown soup in it.
"Enjoy your meal!" she said. Then laughed loudly.
"My partner has a bullet in her arm. You must help her!" begged Hunter.
"Well, she won't be around for long, then, will she?" the woman replied dryly. "It'll save money on food." With the point of her shoe she knocked over one of the bowls. The soup disappeared into the straw. She laughed loudly and left.
"I told you. These guys don't care about anything," said Carter

sadly. He sounded so sorry for himself that the agent grabbed him by the collar and shouted:
"I've had enough. You can whine as much as you want. But only when we get out of here. You'll have to explain a few things then anyway, I think."
"But I don't know anything."
Agnes groaned again. "Boys, do something, for God's sake!"

Übung 70: Wie heißt das Wort auf Englisch?

ÜBUNG 70 !

1. lachen ____________
2. Schüssel ____________
3. Tablett ____________
4. stöhnen ____________
5. jammern ____________
6. Kragen ____________

Hunter rushed over to her. He put his hand on her forehead. It was hot. He carefully removed the bandage she had put around the wound. It was a paper towel from the laboratory and it was now sticky with blood, and stiff. The edges of the wound were already starting to get inflamed. Hunter put the bandage back. He did not have a fresh one with him. He had nothing with him except his suit.
"Help me," he ordered Carter. He pushed the broken rake into Carter's hand and together they started work on the back wall of the room. Through the gaps in the wooden wall, Hunter could see there were open fields behind the shed.
He had to escape and bring reinforcements. Agnes had to get out and see a doctor, nothing else was important.

ÜBUNG 71 !

Übung 71: Vervollständigen Sie die englischen Redewendungen mit den folgenden Wörtern!
(cool, drunk, pretty, quick, thin, wise)

1. as ____________________ as an owl

2. as ____________________ as a rake

3. as ____________________ as a lord

4. as ____________________ as a flash

5. as ______________ as a cucumber

6. as __________________ as a picture

It was already early afternoon when they finally managed to loosen one of the wooden boards. Their guards had not looked in since they had brought the soup. They would probably not come before evening. Hunter would escape from the shed and get reinforcements. He would then come back with them, or alone if he had to. It could be dangerous if the kidnappers noticed he had gone. They would probably call for support, too, and become more violent. The agent did not want to risk that.

He squeezed through the hole in the wall. Agnes was asleep. He told the director to look after her. Then he ran across the field behind the shed. He reached the first greenhouse and hid in the shade. He had a short rest. The effort had made him dizzy. He had not eaten or drunk anything since yesterday. They had not tried any of the soup from the guards.

Without losing any more time, he ran further. He ducked behind the greenhouses. Then he crossed a couple of open fields until he got to another greenhouse. It was Saturday. There was no one there. He

looked through the windows. Rows and rows of vegetable plants. Big red tomatoes hung from green stems.
"And it's the middle of winter!" he thought bitterly. The tomatoes were as big as bowling balls. The red glowed and they were perfectly formed. Bright orange pumpkins were growing behind the tomatoes. It was clear to the agent that nature was certainly being given a helping hand here. A blind man could see that.
He had no time to think about such things. His stomach was aching, he was really hungry. But he did not dare to take anything from the greenhouses. These vegetables were scary.

Übung 72: Markieren Sie! Richtig ✔ oder falsch –?

ÜBUNG 72 !

1. Es war Mittag, als Hunter entkam. ☐
2. Er musste zuerst über ein offenes Feld laufen. ☐
3. Die Geiselnehmer sahen ihn sofort und rannten hinterher. ☐
4. Hunter aß eine Tomate aus dem Treibhaus. ☐
5. Das Gemüse war genmanipuliert. ☐
6. Es war Sonntag. ☐
7. Hunter ging es schlecht, weil er nichts gegessen hatte. ☐

He continued jogging. He heard the sound of tyres on the road behind him. Where could he hide? He was already a hundred metres from the last greenhouse and in the middle of an open field. Without hesitating, he threw himself down onto the ground. From the corner of his eye he saw the off-road vehicle drive past a short distance away. He stayed on the ground until he could not hear the car anymore. He had to be more careful!
His legs started to get heavy, but he had only reached the edge of suburb. Everything was quiet. He once saw a car parked in a drive.

There was a light in the window on the ground floor. He did not dare to ring the bell.
People would probably think he was a beggar from the way he looked. Or an escaped prisoner or a madman. He must have looked very strange running along the road past all the beautiful gardens.

ÜBUNG 73

Übung 73: Wie lauten die Sätze in der richtigen Reihenfolge?

1. field anywhere Hunter hide the in couldn't.

____

2. the past along him car road drove the.

____

3. thought madman like Hunter looked he a.

____

4. help telephone where he for could?

____

5. he to for needed reinforcements ask.

____

Finally he saw a petrol station. He asked the cashier for the nearest telephone. The man behind the counter looked at him confused, then pointed at a door. Hunter thanked him.
"What a car!" said the man. Through the window he was looking at an off-road vehicle which was stopping at one of the petrol pumps. The agent looked.
"But my God, are they expensive." The man behind the counter

whistled. While he was talking and looking out of the window, Hunter stuffed a few chocolate bars into his pocket. He also took a handful of chewing gum and disappeared through the door.
Behind the door there was a kind of storeroom. A telephone hung on the wall next to a brush and a bucket. Hunter had no change. He pulled the telephone casing off and played with a few wires. He had a connection in no time. He dialled a number. At the same time he ripped open one of the chocolate bars with his teeth.

Übung 74: Was gehört zusammen? Ordnen Sie zu!

1. chewing	☐ attendant
2. chocolate	☐ barrel
3. telephone	☐ park
4. petrol pump	☐ windows
5. off-road	☐ bowl
6. gun	☐ bar
7. paper	☐ vehicle
8. electric	☐ gum
9. car	☐ connection
10. soup	☐ cup

He was still chewing the chocolate bar when Emmerson answered in London:
"God, Hunter, where are you? You've got two more cards from Horn. It must be love!"
Hunter interrupted him angrily. With his mouth full, he said, "Emmerson, get me Callaghan. It's very important."
"Important, I see, I see," joked his colleague, and connected him quickly to Callaghan.

Callaghan was angry at being disturbed. Before the agent could tell his story, she shouted at him. Absent from work, no reports about the case, and 17 more deaths, nine of them in England alone.
Hunter interrupted her. he asked for back-up and told her where he was. She did not seem to be listening. Why was he working abroad without telling her? What did he mean, back-up? It was his case, so he should do it alone. Anyway, he had Westcombe.
The agent was furious and tried to interrupt her. He suddenly saw a gun pointing at his face.
"Say goodbye to mummy!" the person said. He knew the voice, it was the Dutchman who had treated Carter so badly. Hunter hung up the telephone.
"That's a good boy!" said the man. "And now we two are going to walk out of here nice and calmly."

ÜBUNG 75 !

Übung 75: Ordnen Sie das Buchstabenchaos zu sinnvollen Wörtern!

He 1. sehpud ________ (schob) Hunter in front of him 2. hotugrh ________ (durch) the door. The pistol was still pointed in his back, but he hid it under his coat.

He made things sound normal by saying to the man behind the 3. tonecru ________ (Theke):

"You know, my brother here has been like this since childhood. Not enough oxygen to the 4. irbna ______ (Hirn) when he was born. He's been mad ever since. Today he thinks he's Batman."

He pulled at Hunter's suit. The man behind the counter 5. ldsime ________ (lächelte), but said nothing. Outside a car drove up. Two 6. plmecneio ____________ (Polizisten) got out. They went into the petrol station. One of them was laughing and telling a story about someone called van Dyck. His colleague glanced at Hunter. The agent tried to get their attention by winking. The pistol was still in his 7. ckab ____________ (Rücken).

The story was interrupted when one of the policemen ordered something. The other one looked at Hunter again, then turned and said, "The same for me, please."

Outside, Hunter was hit hard in the face. Then again. The man pushed him against the car. The agent's hips slammed so hard against the metal that it hurt.
"What the hell were you doing?" the man yelled. "Just because Turner wants you alive doesn't mean we do."
The policemen came back out. Loaded up with food and drink they went over to their car. The man had moved quickly next to Hunter and he smiled at the policemen. They nodded back.
When their car had left the petrol station, he hit Hunter hard again. This time his knee hit the car. He had to accept the game was over. They needed Carter as a witness, and he did not want to put Agnes in any more danger. He let himself be put on the back seat and they drove back to the farm.

ÜBUNG 76

Übung 76: Welche Wörter gehören zusammen?

1. howl

a) ☐ shout b) ☐ accept c) ☐ kneel

2. nod

a) ☐ back b) ☐ head c) ☐ leg

3. witness

a) ☐ speak b) ☐ believe c) ☐ see

4. hurt

a) ☐ injure b) ☐ vomit c) ☐ shake

Carter groaned when the door opened and Hunter fell onto the ground in front of him. The man kicked him once more, then locked the door. When Hunter had recovered, he saw that the hole in the wall had been blocked up by several metal plates on the outside. This way of escape was closed.

Hunter first gave the others the chocolate bars from the petrol station. He then told them about what he had done. Agnes seemed to be a little better. She talked a lot in the discussion about the tomatoes and pumpkins. From what Hunter told her, they could only be genetically-modified. Carter agreed. For the last six months, Turner had always delivered vegetables from Holland for the Mealomeal products. They had only started growing in England that winter. And then Turner had these strange ideas. Carter admitted that he had underestimated Turner. When he had first met him eight months ago, no one had said anything about causing people serious damage with the ready-meals.

At that point the director again started to feel sorry for himself. This time it was Agnes who stopped him.
"We'll deal with Turner later! First we have to get out of here. My arm is getting worse. And knowing Callaghan, we'll be here until the cows come home before she sends reinforcements."
"I think so, too," agreed Hunter.
"Yes, sir!" added Agnes. He had not heard that from her for a long time.

Übung 77: Finden Sie die Entsprechungen!

ÜBUNG 77

1. do something until the cows come home	☐ im Adamskostüm sein
2. hit the nail on the head	☐ einen Knüppel zwischen die Beine werfen
3. have a screw loose	☐ etwas machen, bis man schwarz wird
4. be in one's birthday suit	☐ eine Schraube locker haben
5. throw a spanner in the works	☐ den Nagel auf den Kopf treffen

The sun had been gone a long time by the time they heard the locks being opened again.
"Come and get it!" she cried as she came in with the tray. Light streamed in through the door behind her. she looked like a ghost standing in the door frame holding three plates of the same greeny-brown soup. She was amazed when she looked around the room. The girl was lying in the corner. But where were the other two?
She slowly took a step forward. The handle of the broken rake hit

her hard on the back of the head. She staggered. The tray fell out of her hands. It clattered onto the ground.
Agnes jumped up. The woman looked at her angrily. Carter hit her again with the handle. First she tried to protect herself. Then a further hit on the head knocked her unconscious. Hunter had hit her with the iron chain which he had taken from the wall.

ÜBUNG 78

Übung 78: Lesen Sie weiter und unterstreichen Sie die englische Übersetzung!
(1. Schuppen, 2. starrte, 3. Hof, 4. fluchte, 5. Rechen, 6. erschienen, 7. geräuschvoll, 8. Sprung)

The three of them then ran out of the small room. At the main door of the shed they stopped. They peered around. Everything was quiet in the yard. The sound of low voices came from the main building. After a while Hunter realised it was a TV programme.
They crept along the wooden wall of the shed. They reached the end of the building. The car stood in the middle of the yard. In the darkness the could approach it unseen.
At that moment there was shrill cry from behind them. The woman was back on her feet. She was standing in front of the barn and was shouting for the two men. The sound of movement in the house became louder.
Hunter tried the car door. It was locked. He cursed because they had taken his belt with all his tools off him.
“Have you got a hair pin?” he whispered.
Agnes shook her head. Carter passed him the handle of the rake he had brought with him as a weapon. With all their strength they rammed it against the car window. But nothing happened. The woman’s cries were getting louder. The men appeared noisily at the

door of the house. The yard lights came on brightly. But Hunter and Carter did not give up. They hit it hard against the window. A crack appeared. After hitting it again, it smashed.

Übung 79: Setzen Sie die richtige Präposition ein!
(in, into, out, to, up)

1. Hunter took ________ his gun.
2. Agnes put her glasses ________ her bag.
3. Agents always have to get ________ early for work.
4. Hunter and Agnes flew ________ Rotterdam.
5. It's very hard to climb ________ a mountain.
6. They hid ________ the car.
7. The gangsters got ________ of the car.

Hunter put his hand through the hole and opened the door.
The gangsters had seen them when the window smashed and were running towards the car. They were only a few metres away from them. Hunter had already climbed into the car. Agnes followed him. He played with the wires under the steering wheel.
"Come on, start!" he shouted at the car.
A bullet hit the metal of the car, right next to the door, with a bang.
"Carter!" cried Agnes. She moved closer to Hunter to make room for him. Carter crawled into the car. Another shot was fired.
Agnes pulled the material of Carter's top with her uninjured hand. She wanted to help him get in. Her hand touched something warm and wet. She pulled it back in shock.

"Oh my God!" she cried. She lifted Carter's head. His empty eyes stared out.

The engine started.

"Throw him out!" ordered Hunter.

"What?"

Without answering, the agent gave the director's body a push. It slid out of the car. It fell to the ground with a dull thud. Agnes could now close the car door. A bullet hit the metal outside.

! ÜBUNG 80

Übung 80: Haben die Wörter eine ähnliche Bedeutung? Markieren Sie! Richtig ✔ oder falsch – ?

1. accelerate/speed up ☐
2. move closer/approach ☐
3. escape/hesitate ☐
4. dull/bright ☐
5. collide/hit ☐
6. push/press ☐
7. reach/miss ☐

Hunter stepped on the gas. The car accelerated. He headed for the way between the main house and the yard wall and had almost reached it when suddenly a tractor blocked the road. Hunter had no idea where it had so suddenly come from. He stepped on the brake. Next to him, Agnes was thrown forward. She could only stop herself with both hands. She screamed in pain.

The agent put the car into reverse and headed for the middle of the yard. The woman was nowhere to be seen, but one of the men was still standing there. Hunter saw in his mirror that he was aiming a gun at the car.

“Get down!” he cried. Agnes slid down from the seat onto the floor. Hunter did the same. Under the steering wheel he still kept his leg on the accelerator. In the outside mirror he saw that the man had not moved from his place.
The rear windscreen shattered as the first bullet entered. Two more shots followed, and then another bullet came through the hole in the window. This time it flew through the inside of the car, hit the front windscreen and went out. The man aimed at the car again.
Before he could fire, the car had hit him. There was a bang as the car collided with him. A fraction of a second later the tyres went over his body. Hunter hit the brake. He climbed up from the floor and sat back in the driver’s seat. Through the hole in the windscreen he could see the gangster’s body lying in the yard. A short distance away, he could make out the lifeless body of the director.

Übung 81: Wie heißt das Wort auf Deutsch?

1. distance	☐ Bruchteil
2. speed	☐ treten
3. mirror	☐ Entfernung
4. fraction	☐ Lenkrad
5. aim	☐ Knall
6. brake	☐ Geschwindigkeit
7. hole	☐ zielen
8. step	☐ Bremse
9. bang	☐ Spiegel
10. steering wheel	☐ Loch

The tractor had come closer. It was directly between the car and the yard exit. They would have no chance against a heavy tractor.

Hunter looked around. The wall surrounded the yard on all sides. There were only gaps for the house and the shed.

"The shed!" he shouted. He turned the car and headed for the shed door. The woman had come out again. She was standing on wobbly legs holding something threateningly.

The driver of the tractor accelerated, but it was no use. He took out his gun and fired at the car. They had reached the shed. The woman jumped aside, screaming. The wing of the car hit her and threw her to the left. She crashed against the wooden wall. Hunter stepped on the gas again. The car rammed the back wall. Wood splintered and broke open.

The car was through. Without looking back, Hunter drove over the fields. The off-road vehicle's tyres had no problem driving over the hard earth. They passed the greenhouses and finally turned onto the road. They reached the edge of town.

It seemed that no one had chased after them. At least, there was no one following them in the mirror.

ÜBUNG 82 !

Übung 82: Ersetzen Sie das unterstrichene Wort durch das jeweilige Gegenteil!

1. He drove too fast. ____________________
2. He loved the gangsters. ____________________
3. Hunter locked the door. ____________________
4. His equipment was really heavy. ____________________
5. Hunter agreed with Agnes. ____________________
6. Carter was dead. ____________________

7. It was likely to happen. ______________________

8. The woman was thrown to the left. ______________________

Hunter slowed down to normal speed. He wanted to avoid being stopped by the police for speeding.
"Unless they're all as good at fighting crime as those two at the petrol station," he thought. He smiled. When he looked over Agnes, he stopped smiling. He asked her worriedly if she was all right. She had climbed back onto the seat. She was now leaning on the window. She agreed with his suggestion that they should find a doctor as quickly as possible. But she made one condition, "Take me to Amsterdam. A friend of mine works in a clinic there."
Hunter pointed out that they would need to get to Amsterdam. But she insisted. Holland wasn't that big. They'd soon get there.
He checked the petrol gauge and agreed to do what she said. The car had almost a full tank.

Übung 83: Welche Übersetzung ist richtig?

ÜBUNG 83 !

1. Er überprüfte, ob er genug Benzin hatte.
   a) ☐ He checked when he had enough petrol.
   b) ☐ He checked if he had enough petrol.
   c) ☐ He checked for he had enough petrol.

2. Ein Freund von mir studiert gerade in England.
   a) ☐ A friend of mine studies in England.
   b) ☐ A friend of mine is study in England.
   c) ☐ A friend of mine is studying in England.

3. Ich hole dir einen Schokoladenriegel.

a) ☐ I got you a chocolate bar.

b) ☐ I'll get you a chocolate bar.

c) ☐ I get you a chocolate bar.

The journey passed in a flash. At first Agnes had slept a little. Hunter had relaxed with some music on the radio. When she woke up, he discussed the situation with her.

"So, we'll try to get back to England. Our next appointment is with Turner again." Hunter paused for a moment. He concentrated on the traffic on the motorway. He moved into the right lane for Amsterdam. Then he said, "To be honest, I'm still not sure how the whole thing hangs together. And now we've lost the person who could have told us. Poor Carter."

Agnes sat up in her seat.

"At least he told us a little about what happened," she said. "While you were away, he spent a bit of time with me in that room. He told me how he had met Turner."

"And?"

"Well, Carter had his own restaurant. It wasn't very successful because he couldn't cook very well. Or at least not well enough. That's why he had the idea of starting his own business making microwave ready-meals."

"Mealomeal," said Hunter.

"That's right. But because he didn't have enough capital himself, he needed a partner. He knew about food, but he knew nothing about finances and accounting, or even about how to run a company, so he looked around for a partner who did. Mealomeal had about 60 employees and had its factory near Birmingham."

"I know, I know!" muttered the agent.

Übung 84: Trifft die Aussage zu? Markieren Sie! Richtig ✔ oder falsch –?

1. They were driving to Rotterdam. ☐
2. They were going to find Agnes's friend. ☐
3. Carter started his restaurant with Turner. ☐
4. Carter was a very good cook. ☐
5. Carter needed more money for his business. ☐
6. Mealomeal's headquarters were in London. ☐

Hunter took the next turn-off.
"Turner promised to boost the company. He brought people with him who set up the laboratories and he imported the basic ingredients like vegetables and cereals from other countries."
"Holland, maybe?" asked Hunter.
"Yes, sir!" laughed Agnes before she went on. "They were planning on starting to grow in England next spring. But then this thing happened. It seems Turner wasn't only working on ideas for genetic manipulation. Maybe something else went wrong. Anyway, people who ate Mealomeal products started to die, and not only in England."
"But I thought Mealomeal was only an English product and wasn't on the European market."
"Oh yes it was," said Tina, "In motorway service stations and petrol station shops."
"What?" he asked, amazed.

Agnes did not know any more about it. And they had to concentrate on the road. It was years since Agnes had visited Pauline in Amsterdam. They went around the same streets a few times. Finally, Agnes thought she recognised the house. Hunter parked the car at the side of the road. They got out. He helped her. When he touched her, he could feel her body was very warm. It was high time she saw a doctor.

Übung 85: Unterstreichen Sie das „schwarze Schaf"!

1. walk, stroll, wander, run
2. hard, complicated, straight, impossible
3. call, whine, cry, whimper
4. growl, shout, whisper, scream
5. amazed, calm, astounded, surprised
6. mirror, wing, seat, butt

Pauline was not at home. It was her shift at the clinic. Hunter and Agnes got back in the car and drove to the hospital. A small, bright red car followed close behind them for a while. A man in a black top was driving. He was wearing dark sunglasses. It was too dark for them that winter evening. Hunter speeded up. He changed lanes to try to lose the car which was following them. He almost drove into the car in front. He had been looking in the rear view mirror for too long.

They took the exit for the hospital. The man in the car had disappeared. Hunter stopped at casualty. He asked the young nurse who came through the door if Pauline was there. The man took them both to a ward on the second floor. Agnes turned down his offer to go directly into casualty. She wanted Pauline.

Übung 86: Enträtseln Sie das Lösungswort!

1. Krankenhaus _ □ _ _ _ _ _ _
2. Spion _ □ _
3. Kleider _ _ _ _ _ □ _
4. unterbrechen _ _ _ _ □ _ _ _ _
5. erstaunt _ _ □ _ _ _
6. Notaufnahme _ _ _ _ _ _ □ _
7. lächeln _ _ □ _ _
8. Briefumschlag _ _ _ _ _ □ _ _
9. wechseln _ _ _ □ _ _

Lösung: _ _ _ _ _ _ _ _ _

The doctor was small and thin. Her blond hair was tied back. She did not ask what had happened. She and Agnes hugged briefly. At that moment Hunter had an idea. He interrupted the two women and spoke to Pauline. "It's really embarrassing, but could you lend me some money? Agnes and I really need some new, less noticeable clothes that no one has seen us in yet."

Pauline did not seem surprised. Without saying a word she turned round and disappeared into one of the rooms. A few moments later she returned with an envelope in her hand. She gave it quietly to Hunter.

Then she touched Agnes lightly on the arm to tell her to come with her. They disappeared into one of the rooms. The door banged closed. Hunter was alone in the corridor.

Because he was sure that the whole thing would take a while, he made his way to the foyer. There was a little kiosk, a café, a hairdresser's and, Hunter was glad to see, a little shop which not only sold nightshirts and pyjamas but also trousers and dresses. Hunter opened the door and went in.

Übung 87: Übersetzen Sie!

1. Er fuhr schnell die Straße entlang.

2. Hunter bog in eine Nebenstraße ab.

3. Sie gingen sofort in die Notaufnahme.

4. Könnten Sie mir 10 Pfund ausleihen?

5. Sie umarmten sich kurz.

6. Sie kam mit einem Umschlag in ihrer Hand wieder.

A short while later he returned to the ward carrying several bags. Agnes was already finished. There was a thick white bandage around her arm. Pauline tried to convince her to stay overnight for observation. Agnes refused. But she accepted her invitation to stay at her flat with Hunter. It seemed that she thought the two of them were a couple.

They really did look like a nice couple, thought Hunter when he saw Agnes in her new clothes. He had not got her size exactly right, but it was not too bad. The trousers were baggy around her legs and the blouse hung over them slightly. She looked like a rapper.

Übung 88: Wie lautet das Verb im Simple Past?

1. hear ______________________
2. hug ______________________
3. swear ______________________
4. try ______________________
5. approach ______________________
6. bite ______________________
7. stab ______________________
8. think ______________________
9. throw ______________________

Before they accepted Pauline's invitation to go to one of the restaurants nearby, Hunter telephoned London. Emmerson answered again when he called the general number for his office.

"Kisses from Kent have arrived. Good old Horn," his colleague joked down the phone. Hunter did not have long. He interrupted Emmerson and asked for Callaghan. She was out of the office. She was supposed to be on her way to Rotterdam with a group of reinforcements, Emmerson informed him.

"Damn!" swore Hunter. What was he supposed to do with a group of reinforcements now? He asked to be connected to his immediate superior, Captain Martens. He promised to inform Callaghan. Maybe he could catch her before she left the British Isles. He said he would call Hunter later.

Übung 89: Lesen Sie weiter und unterstreichen Sie die Gegenteile der folgenden Wörter!

(1. loosely, 2. noise, 3. nowhere, 4. started, 5. stayed, 6. sitting, 7. ugly, 8. wide)

The three of them went off. Pauline led them over beautiful bridges and a maze of little canals. The streets were narrow. There were already Christmas lights everywhere. The pub which the doctor was heading for was in the centre. Before they went in, they stopped on the bridge in front of it. The view was really pretty. They were standing there for a while in silence when a cyclist shot past. He tried to grab Pauline's handbag. She spun round and held the bag tightly. The cyclist lost his balance and fell off. Hunter was beside him in a second. He grabbed him by the shoulder and shook him hard.

The young man could not have been older than seventeen. He stammered an apology. There was a scream behind Hunter. He let go of the thief and spun round. Two men in black suits had taken Agnes and Pauline. They were holding guns at their heads.

Übung 90: Ordnen Sie das Buchstabenchaos zu einem sinnvollen Wort!

1. HBGADAN (Handtasche) ______________________
2. FHETI (Dieb) ______________________
3. PITSUD (blöd) ______________________
4. RNRWOA (eng) ______________________

5. GSLUSSENAS (Sonnenbrille) ____________________

6. RNCIMTSFOEENER (Verstärkung) ____________________

7. BRISNGEMSRAA (peinlich) ____________________

"Men in black suits again," the agent thought. One of them shouted to the young man, "Thanks for the diversion!"
The young man grinned, jumped on his bicycle and rode away.
"Why did you want to leave so soon? Didn't you like the farm?" the other man asked and approached Hunter. The man had pushed up his dark sunglasses onto his head. Hunter then recognised him. It was the person in the small car. So they had been followed.
Hunter raised his hands.
"Hey, guys, what do you want with us?"
"We ask the questions!" shouted the man in front of him.
"Move it, Turner wants to talk to you!"
"Are we going to England?" the agent asked spontaneously.
"Turner's here. He's waiting for you in his organic food shop two streets away!" The man laughed and waved his gun in front of Pauline's face. The other man shouted at him: "We ask the questions!"
"Eh?" said his accomplice stupidly.

Übung 91: Welche Wörter gehören zusammen?

1. accomplice

a) ☐ stranger b) ☐ colleague c) ☐ guy

2. approach

a) ☐ near b) ☐ distant c) ☐ open

3. spontaneous

a) ☐ unbelievable b) ☐ possible c) ☐ quick

4. street

a) ☐ field b) ☐ circle c) ☐ corner

At that moment Agnes elbowed him in the ribs. A shot fired from his gun, but she had already ducked out of the way. She gave a precise kick which knocked him off his feet. He crashed down onto the bridge. Hunter was stunned for a moment. That was a kick from an agent's basic training, so it had been worth it to train her for the mission. Pauline used the confusion which her friend had caused. She had pulled a pepper spray out of her handbag. She sprayed it into the man's face next to her. He screamed. He rubbed his eyes with both hands. At that moment Hunter hit the man so hard that he dropped to the ground. He did not move.

His colleague tried to recover, but Agnes continued kicking him. It looked like she was trying to take revenge for all the pain her arm had given her. She stamped her heels on his hands, his back, and his legs. The man moaned and groaned. She stopped. She picked up his gun off the ground and held it at his head.

! ÜBUNG 92

Übung 92: Welche Wörter sind richtig ✔ und welche sind falsch – buchstabiert?

1. ceiling ☐
2. reinforcments ☐
3. seriously ☐
4. overnight ☐

5. spontaneosly ☐
6. recieve ☐
7. interrupt ☐
8. embarrassing ☐

The man whimpered, but Agnes did not care. She pressed the gun harder and harder to his head.

"Don't do it!" shouted Hunter. "It won't help us, Agnes."
"Yes, sir!" she replied. She put the gun into her pocket. "I'll keep it for Turner."
The man was not moving anymore. He was lying flat on the ground.
"What now?" wondered Hunter. He was not sure if they should wait for Martens's call or do something on their own. But what?
"Let's go to the organic food shop!" commanded Agnes.
"But we haven't got any weapons," said the agent.
She waved the attacker's pistol.
"All right!" agreed Hunter. "But you go home, Pauline. I'm not asking you, I'm ordering you. And if Martens calls, tell him we're at the shop."
Pauline laughed. When she realised the seriousness of the situation, she stopped. She gave Hunter her mobile phone in case he needed it and hugged Agnes goodbye. She disappeared over the bridge in the direction they had come from.

Except for a couple of people who were leaving the restaurant, the street was empty. Hunter looked around carefully.
"Shall we go?" the voice of the biologist said beside him.
Hunter shrugged his shoulders. Since he had been with Agnes, he had had to forget all his plans because everything had happened differently. He followed her.

Übung 93: Wie heißt das Verb auf Englisch?

1. vergessen ______________________
2. verschwinden ______________________
3. sprühen ______________________
4. unterbrechen ______________________
5. flüstern ______________________
6. befehlen ______________________
7. versprechen ______________________

The shop was still open. But it was nearly closing time, and the shop assistant was hurrying a couple of customers to the till. Hunter and Agnes slipped quickly through the door.
"We're closing," the girl said nicely from behind the counter.
"I only need, oh, what was it …," replied Agnes and disappeared between the shelves.
"Could you tell your wife that I really have to close. We're actually closed already."
Hunter also disappeared between the tall shelves. It took a while before he found Agnes. She was standing in front of the fresh vegetables, feeling the oversized, bright red tomatoes. The cucumbers were unusually long and thick. They all looked exactly the same.
When she saw Hunter coming, she rushed to the till with a bottle of salad dressing. With a wink, she dropped the bottle on the floor.
The girl came from the till. Agnes apologised to her. She bent down to help the assistant clean up. Some of the orange sauce got onto her blouse while she was helping.

Übung 94: Wie lauten die Pluralformen der Substantive?

1. shelf ______________________
2. person ______________________
3. copy ______________________
4. potato ______________________
5. mouse ______________________
6. box ______________________
7. tooth ______________________

The girl showed her where the customer toilets were so that she could clean her blouse. Hunter went with her to help. The girl went back to the counter.

The agent and the biologist left the ladies' toilets quickly. Agnes had cleaned off the sauce. They passed crates and boxes which were piled up in the corridor and moved further away from the door of the shop. The offices had to be here at the back somewhere. The corridor was not very long. There were only three doors. Everything was silent. At the end of the corridor they found a metal staircase which went down to the cellar.

The light down there was dim. They tried to find their way as best they could. A few times they walked into crates and boxes which were piled next to the walls. Some of them were wooden and looked like the one Hunter had seen in the plane. He did not try to open them. They had no time to lose.

Übung 95: Setzen Sie die richtige Präposition ein!
(along, around, down, from, in, on)

They could now hear quiet voices. A metal door blocked their path. Several people were talking 1. ______ the other side. Hunter could not understand exactly what they were saying. Someone above shouted "Hello?" twice. It had to be the shop assistant. She must have noticed that they were no longer 2. ______ the toilets.

"She's coming!" whispered Agnes.

She and Hunter looked 3. ______. Next to the door there were a few wooden boxes piled up. That would be a good enough hiding place for the moment. They jumped behind and waited. The girl really was coming 4. ______ the stairs. She hesitated for a moment, then decided to go 5. ______ the corridor. When she reached the metal door, she paused again. She lifted her fist and lowered it again. Then she decided to knock.

The door was pulled open. Someone asked her what she wanted. She shyly told them about the missing customers. The man laughed. Several voices could be heard coming 6. ______ the room. Hunter could make out three. One of the deepest voices seemed to be Turner's.

This voice told the man at the door to go back upstairs with the girl.

The man laughed again. He put his arm 7. ________ the assistant and they walked 8. ________ the corridor. Just before the stairs, he put his hand 9. ________ her bottom. She screamed angrily. There was laughter in the room.

ÜBUNG 96 !

Übung 96: Finden Sie die Synonyme für die Wörter in Klammern!

1. Hunter (went back) ________________ to the laboratory.
2. The woman (shouted) ________ when the man attacked her.
3. Agnes (paused) __________ a moment before she fired.
4. Turner was (furious) ______________ with his men.
5. They both (leaped) ________________ behind the crates.
6. Agnes (noticed) __________ some footprints on the floor.
7. Hunter (arrived at) ___________ the door and pushed it open.

The door now stood open a little. Hunter and Agnes stepped out from their hiding place. They positioned themselves next to the door frame and Agnes passed the gun to Hunter. But he gave it back to her – she would need it more than him. He was fully trained for hand-to-hand combat.
He looked carefully into the room. He saw a table, a card table. There were cards, piles of papers and a lot of money on it. There were also glasses and a couple of revolvers.
There were two men and a woman leaning on the table. So that they would not see him, Hunter quickly moved back behind the door

frame. The footsteps of the man who had gone upstairs with the shop assistant could be heard on the stairs. Agnes and Hunter dashed behind the boxes again. Just before the man reached the door, Hunter jumped up from his hiding place. The man stared at him with his mouth open.

Hunter knocked him out with a blow to the side of his head. The man fell. His massive body thudded onto the stone floor. Hunter immediately jumped back behind the boxes next to Agnes.

A chair was pushed forward in the room. The sound of grumbling got louder. Someone came to the door. It opened wider and a man looked out. When the man saw his colleague on the floor, he rushed over to him. He bent down. Hunter was immediately in position. He gave the man a karate chop to the neck. The fat man fell on top of the other body.

Hunter waved at Agnes. They had to act fast. Hitting was silent and effective, but no one could say how long the men would remain unconscious. Agnes held the gun. Hunter had signalled to her. He wanted to be prepared for any attack. They slowly approached the door.

ÜBUNG 97 !

Übung 97: Was gehört zusammen? Ordnen Sie zu!
(carton, crate, packet, pat, loaf, tin, tub)

1. a ____________________ of beer

2. a ____________________ of butter

3. a ____________________ of crisps

4. a ____________________ of milk

5. a ________________ of ice-cream

6. a ________________ of bread

7. a ________________ of baked beans

The agent reached the door frame. There were still two people in the room – a man with an attractive blonde woman on his knee.

"Did you want to talk to me?" asked Hunter. He signalled to Agnes to stay behind and wait for him. He entered the room alone. The room was filled with smoke. Turner pushed the woman off his knee. She went to the bar at the back of the room.
"A drink?" Turner asked. Hunter said no.
He approached the table. Turner watched him. The agent thought he seemed amused.
"You want to know about us, then?" he said. "Who are you? Police? Secret Service? Or just interested?"
Hunter replied immediately, "Just interested. What do you think?"
"For someone who's just interested, you sniff around a lot."
"Do you think I don't do my homework?" laughed Hunter.
Turner signalled him to sit down. While Hunter sat down, Turner played with the cards in his hand.
"So what do you want?" he asked across the table.
"What have you got?" replied Hunter.
"Are we talking about normal, chemical or biological?"
Hunter had only one answer. "Biological"
"Well, I never. You're one of the worst types. Biological guys do a lot of damage."

Hunter grinned, but said nothing.

ÜBUNG 98

Übung 98: Wie lautet die Steigerungsform der Adjektive?

1. It was the ______________ (bad) mission Hunter had ever had.
2. It was ____________________ (important) to take Agnes to a hospital.
3. Things had to get _________________ (good).
4. Amsterdam is ____________________ (pretty) than Rotterdam.
5. Nothing could be _____________________________________ (simple)!
6. Agnes was _________________________________ (tired) than Hunter.
7. This mission was _________________________ (dangerous) than his last one.

Turner put the cards in a pile on the table. "OK. You want "Tertechs". But that's not possible."
"You mean to tell me I hang around here all this time and you …"
Turner interrupted him. "No, no, don't misunderstand me. I'm very grateful that you took Carter off my hands. Your performance in the farmyard was worth an Oscar. It was a shame about the men, though."
Hunter smiled.
"All right. How much and where?" asked Turner.
"I'm planning something rather big. In Germany."
"Nothing could be simpler! We deliver our tasty "Mealomeal" to petrol stations in Munich, Cologne, Berlin, and Frankfurt. Just say where you want them. You come to the delivery point and the first boxes of ready-meals go to you."
Hunter looked like he did not understand.
"Yes, that's right – ready-meals. The stuff is in the little flavour sachet for the sauce."
Hunter swallowed.

"First you transfer half the money, then we give you the product code of the right crate and the delivery time and location. You pick up the crate at the location. You give the petrol pump attendant the rest of the money in an envelope. And then, have fun!"

"That's a very clever idea!" said Hunter.

"And the best thing is, the ready-meal company is also doing very well because of a few extra big tomatoes!"

Hunter laughed again. Turner picked up the cards in front of him. He threw one into Hunter's face with contempt.

"Got you!" he cried. "Where do you think we are, in a kindergarten?"

Hunter quickly jumped up out of his chair. He reached for one of the guns on the table.

"They're not loaded," shouted the woman from the bar. Hunter pulled the trigger. A click told him the woman was right. He kept hold of the gun anyway. Turner had now stood up. He pulled out his gun and aimed it at the agent.

"How stupid do you think I am?" he said.

"What do you mean? I thought we had a deal," said Hunter. A bullet flew past his ear. The woman screamed. Bottles and glasses exploded as the bullet hit the shelf behind the bar.

Übung 99: Trifft die Aussage zu? Markieren Sie! Richtig ✔ oder falsch –?

ÜBUNG 99 !

1. Turner and Hunter played cards. ☐
2. Deliveries of "Tertechs" happened at petrol stations. ☐
3. People paid all the money for "Tertechs" before the delivery. ☐
4. The "Tertechs" was hidden in the flavour sachet. ☐
5. Turner didn't believe that Hunter wanted to buy "Tertechs". ☐

6. Turner's shot injured Hunter. ☐
7. Hunter's gun didn't have any bullets. ☐

Hunter moved back. He held both his hands up. He still had the empty gun in one hand. He heard steps coming along the corridor. The shop assistant appeared at the door. She asked for the keys because she wanted to lock the offices.
Turner put his gun down. He laughed loudly, patted Hunter on the shoulder and introduced Hunter to the girl – as his new business partner. Hunter knew why Turner was playing this game. Nevertheless, he smiled at the girl. Turner put his gun on the table.
Turner told her that he would lock up himself. He still had things to discuss with Hunter. The girl left, but stopped just in front of the door. She was staring at something. She looked around at her boss. He went quickly to the door to see what was there.
Agnes was standing ready in the door. She aimed her gun at the gangster. He was speechless for a moment. Then he grabbed the shop assistant and used her as a human shield between himself and Agnes. He moved slowly towards the stairs. One of his hands was around the girl's throat. He squeezed. She started choking.
Agnes kept them both in her sights. Hunter came to help.

ÜBUNG 100 !

Übung 100: Ordnen Sie die Wörter den richtigen Überbegriffen zu!

a) gun
b) cereal
c) worried
d) cucumber
e) lockpick
f) knife

i) nurse
j) pumpkin
k) syringe
l) assistant
m) amazed
n) codebreaker

g) screen
h) stunned
o) pepper spray
p) caretaker

1. Gefühle ______

2. Lebensmittel ______

3. Waffen ______

4. Technik ______

5. Menschen ______

There was a thud as the woman at the bar fell off her stool. She had clearly had too much to drink. Hunter ran to the back of the room, grabbed her arm, and dragged her into the corridor. He took Agnes's gun and aimed it at the woman. Turner stood still.
"Shoot her, the drunken cow!" he cried. He had almost reached the stairs. The woman Hunter was holding was not going to ignore Turner's insult. She freed herself and stormed down the corridor after him. Heavy footsteps came down the stairs. About ten men appeared. They were all wearing black suits and had guns. Turner pushed the girl away. She hit the wall hard. She stood still, crying. Turner shouted angrily at the men for coming so late. He asked Kevin why. He explained that he had been with his men in England. The blonde woman had reached Turner. "Drunken cow!" she cried and slapped him across the face. She was hit in the head by a bullet. She looked at Turner confused for a moment. Then she fell dead to the floor.
"Sorry, boss!" said the gunman.
"If only you were always so fast!" Turner turned round.
"And now you two."
Hunter and Agnes had disappeared.

Übung 101: Unterstreichen Sie die englische Übersetzung der folgenden Wörter!
(1. suchen, 2. kroch, 3. schrie, 4. Schmerz, 5. sofort, 6. kämpften, 7. Schuss, 8. rieb)

Chaos followed. Turner gave the order to search for them. His men went along the corridor and looked in the room with the card table. One of them crawled behind the boxes.
Agnes and Hunter stayed perfectly still. They were hiding behind the bar. Agnes had the gun again. Hunter had a broken bottle.
He quickly attacked when the first man bent over the bar. The bottle cut open his cheek. He fell back. He screamed. One of his colleagues heard him and ran to him. a bullet from Agnes's gun hit him in the shoulder. He moved back, howling in pain, but immediately came back and started firing angrily at the two under the bar. Agnes and Hunter ducked under the bar. The attacker jumped onto the counter. Before he could jump to the other side, Hunter had jumped up and dragged him by the arm onto the floor. They struggled with each other.
Agnes had to deal with the next one who had jumped over the bar. His shot missed her by an inch. She fired back, but her shot went past him. Before he could shoot again, Agnes had thrown a cocktail shaker at him. The metal shaker hit him hard on the head. He rubbed his head angrily. She fired.

There was now more noise at the door. Shots hit the walls. People shouted. Agnes looked at Hunter, but he was still fighting the man on the floor. The pieces of glass under their bodies crunched. She rolled under the counter towards Hunter. He was now lying underneath and the other man was sitting on him. He was kneeling on the agent's arms and aiming at his chest.

"No!" shouted Agnes. Her shot went through the man's head. He collapsed and buried Hunter underneath him. Hunter crawled out with difficulty.
"Thanks!"

Übung 102: Bilden Sie Genitiv-Konstruktionen!

1. Hunter/gun ____________________
2. the gangsters/hideout ____________________
3. people/lives ____________________
4. Callaghan/office ____________________
5. Martin and Julia/flat ____________________
6. children/toys ____________________
7. the plane/wheels ____________________

They both took their positions again behind the bar. They waited for the next one to come. But no one appeared. It had suddenly become very quiet. How could that be?
The strange silence continued. The agent slowly looked over the bar. He looked over quickly and ducked back down. The room was full of people but no one was speaking.
"Helene, don't you remember me?" asked Turner.
"No, Turner, I've never seen you before."
Hunter recognised the voice. It could not be true. A shot hit the cellar roof with a thud. Chaos broke out again. Hunter and Agnes came out from their cover. Turner must have injured Callaghan. She was holding her leg. Her gun lay on the floor a short distance away. Too far to reach.

Übung 103: Enträtseln Sie das Lösungswort!

1. Angriff _ _ _ _ _ ☐
2. mischen _ ☐ _
3. entwickeln ☐ _ _ _ _ _ _
4. eintreten _ ☐ _ _ _
5. dunkel _ ☐ _ _
6. wiederholen _ _ ☐ _ _ _
7. Probe _ _ _ ☐ _ _
8. zweite _ ☐ _ _ _ _
9. gerade _ _ ☐ _ _ _ _ _

Lösung: _ _ _ _ _ _ _ _ _

A second later the chaos stopped again. Turner approached Callaghan, who was sitting on the floor in front of him. He waved his gun in front of her eyes. His men behind formed a semi-circle. Callaghan's people stood like a wall behind her. Both sides were aiming their guns at each other.
"My dear Helene, you don't want to pretend you don't know me. Or don't you recognise me anymore because it's been such a long time since we saw each other?"
"Shut up!" she said through her teeth.
"Darling, that's not a very nice thing to say!" he replied. "You sounded much different at the police academy. But then you had to join the Secret Service."

Übung 104: Was gehört zusammen? Ordnen Sie zu!

1. company	☐ shaker
2. gun	☐ food

3. cocktail ☐ shield
4. card ☐ partner
5. bottle ☐ headquarters
6. organic ☐ delivery
7. business ☐ barrel
8. human ☐ opener
9. special ☐ table

He stood directly over her. He made his gun ready with a click. He had her forehead exactly in his sights. She looked at him directly in the eye.
There was a single bang. Turner touched the back of his neck. He brought his hand forward again and looked at it – blood. He looked at Callaghan in disbelief. He tried to aim his gun at her. Time seemed to slow down. They both stared at each other without moving. He collapsed.

ÜBUNG 105 !

Übung 105: Setzen Sie die Verben ein!
(arrested, came, limped, needed, panicked, said, started, thanked)

His people (1. gerieten in Panik) ______________ and (2. fingen an) ______________ to run around or shoot. Callaghan's expert team (3. brauchten) ______________ a few minutes to get the situation under control. They then (4. verhafteten) ______________ Turner's people.
Hunter and Agnes (5. kam) ______________ around from the bar. Callaghan had got up. She was wearing a dark special opera-

tions fighting suit and she (6. humpelte) ______________ over to them.

“Thank you!” she (7. sagte) ______________ to Hunter. He pointed at his partner.

“Westcombe fired.”

“Yes, sir!”

Callaghan (8. dankte) ______________ her.

The biologist turned down the offer to transfer to Operations.

ÜBUNG 106

Übung 106: Wie heißt das Wort auf Deutsch?

1. bandage ______________
2. to insult ______________
3. injured ______________
4. forehead ______________
5. to collapse ______________
6. to aim ______________
7. confused ______________

Pauline had not only explained to Captain Martens on the telephone where the support team would find Agnes and Hunter, she had also helped the injured. In front of the organic food shop, there were ambulances which were looking after the wounded.

When Callaghan had learnt who this Turner was, she had decided to lead the special commando herself. She had disliked the man when she was younger. Hunter had never imagined she could be so brave. Like Agnes, she did not complain about her injury. The two women stood side by side – one of them with a bandage around her shoulder, the other with one around her leg. Hunter joined them.

Übung 107: Unterstreichen Sie die Übersetzungen der folgenden Wörter!
(1. Zwischenhändler, 2. überrascht, 3. gesund, 4. versiegelt, 5. vergiftete, 6. tödlich, 7. grinste, 8. Flüssigkeit)

"So they smuggled the biological weapons in their ready-meals," Callaghan concluded from Agnes's story.
"Exactly. It seems some of it leaked into the food. That's what poisoned the victims. The stuff is lethal!"
Hunter tapped Agnes on her healthy shoulder. "Westcombe, you've surprised me!"
"And me, too," added the boss.
"And you surprised me, Hunter."
They all laughed. Callaghan left them for a moment. She had to report to London. The Secret Service had to inform all the international authorities to remove all Mealomeal products from the shelves.
"The question is whether Turner was a middleman or whether he made and sold this "Tertechs" himself," wondered Hunter.
"We'll see. Check how old the stuff here is and if it's really the same as the original "Tertechs" from the 1980s," replied Agnes.
She grinned as she took a sealed test tube out of her trouser pocket. There was a yellow liquid in it.

"Is that …?" Hunter began to ask, amazed.
"Exactly, from Lab 1. Just don't ask where I hid it.

! ÜBUNG 108

Übung 108: Gibt der Satz den richtigen Sachverhalt wieder? Markieren Sie! Richtig ✔ oder falsch – ?

1. Callaghan knew who Turner was. ☐
2. Callaghan and Turner were good friends in the past. ☐
3. Hunter shot Turner. ☐
4. Everyone expected Agnes to be such a good agent. ☐
5. It was an accident that the "Tertechs" got into the Mealomeal. ☐
6. "Tertechs" was originally a biological weapon from the 1970s. ☐
7. Agnes had kept a test tube of "Tertechs" all the time. ☐

"So this Turner agreed to be a partner in Carter's company, which was almost bankrupt?" Percy asked. They were sitting at Hunter's desk and the young agent was trying to ask about every little detail of what had happened. Hunter continued, "Exactly. They wanted to develop biological weapons using the food company as a cover. The stuff's called "Tertechs". It was around in the 1980s. The stuff was delivered to the buyer in the packaging of a ready-meal."
"What a disguise!" said Percy.

! ÜBUNG 109

Übung 109: Übersetzen Sie!

1. Gut gemacht!

____

2. „Tertechs" wurde in den 80er Jahren als Biowaffe entwickelt.

____

3. Die Firma war fast pleite.

4. Als er jung war, wollte er Polizist werden.

5. Callaghan tat so, als ob sie Turner nicht erkennen würde.

A cough interrupted them. "Hunter, not a bad job. Captain Martens is expecting you this afternoon at a meeting about the job in the Pacific."
Callaghan pushed out her chest and looked the agent squarely in the eye.
"Was that praise?" Hunter asked.
"If you wanted me to praise you, you would have made sure that young witness wasn't blown up by amateur arms dealers. And you wouldn't have carried out an operation abroad without my permission. And you wouldn't have let a whole support team have to look for you for hours. You wouldn't have caught just a small fry like Turner, but also a few more of the people at the top."

Hunter interrupted her. "You're our expert on arms dealing." The effect of his words could clearly be seen on her face. He suddenly felt sorry he had said them. Maybe she was not all that bad, he thought as he remembered their joint operation.

Her mouth tensed. Her eyebrows narrowed. She continued slowly: "Just be glad nothing happened to Westcombe – like little Gina in Italy." With that she turned and left.
"Maybe she is that bad after all," Hunter thought.

Übung 110: Beantworten Sie die Fragen zum Text!

1. Where will Hunter's next mission be?

2. How did Turner smuggle the "Tertechs"?

3. Did Turner plan to kill people?

4. What part of Callaghan's body was injured?

5. Where did Callaghan first meet Turner?

"That told her," said Percy happily. When he heard about Agnes's injury, he stopped being jealous of her. He had been afraid that she might become Hunter's new partner.
"How's the biologist?" he asked his boss.
"Better, and tonight even better." Percy looked at him astonished. Hunter explained. "I've invited her to dinner."
"Can you cook?" asked Percy.
"Of course. Macaroni cheese. Guaranteed not to contain products which haven't been genetically-modified. At least, that's what it says on the box."
"Sounds worse than the food at the training camp," said Percy before he could stop himself. Then he suddenly remembered. "Do you know where I was?"

Hunter looked at him, confused. Before he could answer, the young man couldn't hold the suspense any longer. "Kentucky!"

Abschlusstest

Übung 1: Nennen Sie ein Synonym für die folgenden Wörter!

1. to rush ____________________
2. to say again ____________________
3. to say sorry ____________________
4. to turn around quickly ____________________
5. to vanish ____________________
6. to creep ____________________
7. to peer ____________________

Übung 2: Ordnen Sie das Buchstabenchaos zu sinnvollen Wörtern!

1. LDAREE (Händler) ____________________
2. CPISETAR (üben) ____________________
3. EIPSBLSOMI (unmöglich) ____________________
4. YIJNRU (Verletzung) ____________________
5. CLPOADK (Vorhängeschloss) ____________________
6. LSJEAUO (eifersüchtig) ____________________
7. UTGEDEANRA (garantiert) ____________________

Übung 3: Welche Wörter gehören zusammen?

1. limp

a) ☐ arm   b) ☐ neck   c) ☐ leg

2. lock

a) ☐ corridor b) ☐ door c) ☐ hospital

3. science

a) ☐ spy b) ☐ biologist c) ☐ painter

4. hospital

a) ☐ ward b) ☐ fire c) ☐ guard

Übung 4: Übersetzen Sie und enträtseln Sie das Lösungswort!

1. entscheiden _ ☐ _ _ _ _
2. sich beeilen _ _ ☐ _
3. Kürbis _ _ _ ☐ _ _ _
4. klein _ ☐ _ _ _ _
5. Befehl ☐ _ _ _ _
6. Granate _ _ _ ☐ _ _ _
7. Bauernhof _ ☐ _ _ _ _ _ _
8. zustimmen _ ☐ _ _ _
9. winken _ _ _ ☐

Lösung: _ _ _ _ _ _ _ _ _

Übung 5: Wie lauten die Sätze in der richtigen Reihenfolge?

1. off the fast plane took.

____

2. the of Hunter fast out room went.

____

3. borrow 25 I you from can pounds?

4. best was agent the Hunter service in secret the.

Übung 6: Unterstreichen Sie die richtige Alternative!

1. Can you speak/talk Dutch?
2. Can you tell/say me the way to Amsterdam?
3. You have to pull/press the button.
4. Agnes had to where/wear a special suit for the mission.
5. Her trousers were very loose/lose.
6. I'm a big amateur/fan of spy stories!

Übung 7: Setzen Sie die richtige Form des Simple Past ein!

They both 1. __________ (to take) their positions again behind the bar. They 2. __________ (to wait) for the next one to come. But no one 3.__________(to come). It suddenly 4.__________ (to become) very quiet. Why 5. __________ (to be) that?

The strange silence 6. __________ (to carry on). The agent slowly 7.__________ (to look) over the bar and quickly 8.__________ (to duck) back down. The room was full of people but no one 9. __________ (to speak). Hunter 10. __________ (to leap) up.

Übung 8: Beantworten Sie die Fragen zum Text!

1. Which part of the secret service did Agnes come from?

2. What was in the ammunition box in the plane?

3. How did Hunter and Carter make a hole in the farm shed?

4. Why did Hunter think Agnes looked like a rapper in the hospital?

5. Where did Agnes's bullet hit Turner?

Übung 9: Übersetzen Sie!

1. Hunter sagte, es wäre zu riskant, mit Agnes einzubrechen.

2. Das Flugzeug ist sofort zurück nach England geflogen.

3. Sehe ich aus wie ein Idiot?

4. Der Wachmann warf eine Granate und sprengte das Auto in die Luft.

5. Callaghan kannte Turner seit der Polizeiakademie.

Übung 10: Welches Wort ist richtig ✔ und welches ist falsch – buchstabiert?

1. inconveninent ☐
2. especially ☐
3. combination ☐
4. casuality ☐
5. hapiness ☐
6. remembered ☐
7. intelligense ☐

Übung 11: Wie heißt das Wort auf Deutsch?

1. distance	☐ Bruchteil
2. speed	☐ treten
3. mirror	☐ Entfernung
4. fraction	☐ Lenkrad
5. aim	☐ Knall
6. brake	☐ Geschwindigkeit
7. hole	☐ zielen
8. step	☐ Bremse
9. bang	☐ Spiegel
10. steering wheel	☐ Loch

Lösungen

Übung 1: 1. Kopf 2. Rücken 3. Bein 4. Stirn 5. Augenbraue 6. Wange 7. Hals
Übung 2: 1.thin 2. slow 3. happy 4. short 5. strong 6. thin 7. cold
Übung 3: 1. out 2. from 3. to 4. off 5. at 6. on 7. on
Übung 4: 1. policeman 2. teacher 3. secretary 4. lawyer 5. dentist 6. caretaker
Übung 5: 1. went 2. came 3. watched 4. saw 5. found 6. had 7. entered
Übung 6: 1. cosy 2. interrupt 3. sympathetic 4. lipstick 5. desk 6. worried
Übung 7: 1. answer/reply 2. say/speak 3. give/pass 4. stop/pause 5. want/need 6. call/telephone 7. cry/shout 8. finish/end
Übung 8: 1. Hunter worked for the secret service. 2. He was happy to work in Operations. 3. He had lived there for a few years. 4. Percy wanted to learn more about his job. 5. He was sad the girl in Italy was dead. 6. He knew about Callaghan's illegal activities.
Übung 9: Hunter was envious of Emmerson. 2. He shared the office with twenty other colleagues. 3. Callaghan was wearing dark lipstick. 4. His job was top secret. 5. I'll send you a postcard!
Übung 10: 1. invite 2. leather 3. neighbour 4. apologise 5. somewhere 6. equipment
Übung 11: 1. falsch 2. falsch 3. richtig 4. falsch 5. richtig 6. falsch 7. richtig
Übung 12: 1. staff/entrance 2. machine/gun 3. car/key 4. ground/floor 5. shop/assistant 6. microwave/oven 7. arms/deal 8. bar/stool 9. mobile/phone 10. training/camp
Übung 13: 1. on 2. in 3. in 4. in 5. at 6. on 7. at
Übung 14: 1. bunch 2. loaf 3. pint 4. bundle 5. pack 6. crowd 7. queue
Übung 15: 1. loud/quiet 2. interesting/boring 3. ordinary/strange 4. bright/dim 5. polite/rude 6. best/worst 7. upright/bent 8. confident/shy 9. tense/relaxed 10. freezing/boiling
Übung 16: 1. A bank and financial consultancy. 2. To the underground station. 3. He turned around, ducked and kicked him. 4. Ted. 5. The man in the car.
Übung 17: 1. apparently 2. richtig 3. successful 4. richtig 5. richtig 6. vegetable 7. richtig
Übung 18: 1. unlock 2. disagree 3. inexperienced 4. impolite 5. impossible 6. uncover 7. uncomfortable
Übung 19: 1. breath 2. crumpled 3. knelt 4. swallowed 5. drawers 6. screamed
Übung 20: 1. strength 2. happiness 3. silence 4. mixture 5. death 6. amazement
Übung 21: 1. cleaned 2. angry 3. shot 4. crazy 5. hurried
Übung 22: 1. wrist 2. registration 3. bulb 4. handle 5. colleague 6. neighbour
Übung 23: 1. make 2. do 3. do 4. make 5. do 6. do 7. do 8. make
Übung 24: 1. lunch 2. laboratory 3. similar 4. strange 5. vomit 6. calm
Übung 25: 1. b 2. c 3. a
Übung 26: 1. hung 2. left 3. was 4. jumped 5. waved 6. rubbed 7. pulled 8. was 9. wanted 10. went
Übung 27: 1. expensive/teuer 2. conspicuous/auffällig 3. outline/Abriss 4. mist/

Nebel 5. muffled/gedämpft 6. confidence/Selbstvertrauen 7. baggy/ausgeleiert 8. accelerate/beschleunigen 9. pace/Lauftempo 10. encouraging/ermutigend

Übung 28: 1. encourage 2. bother 3. delicate 4. drive 5. baggy 6. belt 7. gun

Übung 29: 1. lose 2. broke 3. parked 4. fiddled 5. started 6. forced 7. sounded 8. changed 9. reached 10. accelerated

Übung 30: 1. whirr 2. overtake 3. tyre 4. lane

Übung 31: 1. comfortable 2. nervous 3. sympathetic 4. peaceful 5. suspicious 6. successful

Übung 32: 1. einen Verdacht haben 2. sich etwas von der Seele reden 3. sich lächerlich machen 4. jemandem auf die Nerven gehen 5. ein Geschick für etwas haben 6. ins Fettnäpfchen treten 7. jemanden von der kurzen Leine lassen 8. jemandem die Hölle heiß machen

Übung 33: 1. attack 2. practice 3. target 4. syringe 5. attempt 6. pocket 7. climb

Übung 34: 1. falsch 2. falsch 3. richtig 4. falsch 5. richtig 6. richtig

Übung 35: 1. Hunter found a postcard on his desk. 2. The report gave him more information. 3. It could have been an allergic reaction. 4. No one really knew where it had come from. 5. Hunter didn't really believe any of the possibilities.

Übung 36: 1. over 2. on 3. off 4. out 5. off 6. out

Übung 37: 1. trace 2. ready-meal 3. surprised 4. question 5. genetic 6. gun 7. abbreviation 8. case Lösung: test tube

Übung 38: 1. hide 2. darkness 3. whole 4. barbed wire 5. discovered 6. estate car 7. tools 8. clumsily

Übung 39: 1. slowly 2. strangely 3. brightly 4. unusually 5. fast 6. carefully 7. early

Übung 40: 1. They jogged along the path. 2. With an electricity detector. 3. No. 4. Hunter cut a hole with metal cutters. 5. No. 6. A three-metre high wall.

Übung 41: 1. He checked if the fence was safe. 2. The gate was locked 3. They planned to break into the building. 4. Hunter jumped easily over the wall. 5. The bright moonlight was dangerous for the mission.

Übung 42: 1. b 2. b 3. c

Übung 43: 1. beam 2. screen 3. factory 4. whisper 5. laboratory

Übung 44: 1. lose 2. shade 3. nice 4. big 5. current 6. sensitive 7. salary

Übung 45: 1. unzip 2. irrelevant 3. unpleasant 4. improbable 5. indirect 6. unfortunate 7. irresponsible

Übung 46: 1. was 2. were 3. covered 4. knew 5. whispered 6. turned 7. went 8. came 9. saw 10. knelt

Übung 47: 1. ceiling 2. cellar 3. opposite 4. crawl 5. blind 6. dust 7. cobweb 8. heel 9. welding torch 10. buzz

Übung 48: 1. Because the guards might see it on the camera. 2. Because they were made of an unbreakable material. 3. With a codebreaker. 4. Because he wanted to find the camera. 5. He cut the cable.

Übung 49: 1. knife 2. loner 3. necessary 4. plane 5. pineapple 6. throat 7. creep

Übung 50: 1. Hunter found the man under the table. 2. He untied the rope around his hands. 3. Please don't hurt me anymore. 4. He asked the man what he was doing there. 5. He told the man he was an agent.
Übung 51: 1. fast 2. repeated 3. thin 4. pulled 5. honest
Übung 52: 1. TV/screen 2. test/tube 3. open-plan/office 4. toilet/seat 5. kitchen/table 6. frozen/food 7. coffee/machine 8. combination/lock
Übung 53: 1. safety 2. secret 3. breathe 4. whisper 5. guard 6. torch 7. disappear 8. noise 9. beam Lösung: staircase
Übung 54: 1. c 2. a 3. b 4. c
Übung 55: 1. asked 2. careful 3. remains 4. pieces 5. footsteps 6. boxes 7. enough 8. cabinet
Übung 56: 1. falsch 2. richtig 3. richtig 4. falsch 5. richtig 6. richtig
Übung 57: 1. b 2. a 3. b
Übung 58: 1. slid 2. shot 3. stood 4. became 5. hit 6. apologised 7. bent
Übung 59: 1. tomorrow 2. prisoner 3. threaten 4. outside 5. direction 6. concrete 7. scream
Übung 60: 1. richtig 2. falsch 3. falsch 4. richtig 5. falsch
Übung 61: 1. on 2. in 3. in 4. through 5. of 6. from 7. to 8. at 9. out 10. out
Übung 62: 1. easy 2. light 3. increase 4. leave 5. late 6. bottom 7. dangerous
Übung 63: 1. left 2. ideas 3. now 4. save 5. quiet 6. anything
Übung 64: 1. Agnes fell asleep quickly. 2. Hunter untied the rope first. 3. Hurry up! 4. The floor of the plane was very cold. 5. The plane took off slowly.
Übung 65: 1. Flugzeug/plane 2. packen/grab 3. Strahl/ray 4. Munition/ammunition 5. vorwärts/forwards 6. Mut/bravery 7. sich beeilen/hurry 8. schlagen/punch 9. wimmern/whimper 10. merken/notice
Übung 66: 1. prisoner 2. hangar 3. bullet 4. runway 5. butt
Übung 67: 1. b 2. c 3. c
Übung 68: 1. ropes 2. wooden walls 3. straw 4. gap 5. belt 6. anaesthetic 7. emergency
Übung 69: 1. agree 2. bullet 3. wound 4. shoulder 5. tie 6. chain 7. escape 8. shed Lösung: genetics
Übung 70: 1. laugh 2. bowl 3. tray 4. groan 5. whine 6. collar
Übung 71: 1. wise 2. thin 3. drunk 4. quick 5. cool 6. pretty
Übung 72: 1. falsch 2. richtig 3. falsch 4. falsch 5. richtig 6. falsch 7. richtig
Übung 73: 1. Hunter couldn't hide anywhere in the field. 2. The car drove past him along the road. 3. Hunter thought he looked like a madman. 4. Where could he telephone for help? 5. He needed to ask for reinforcements.
Übung 74: 1. chewing/gum 2. chocolate/bar 3. telephone/connection 4. petrol pump/attendant 5. off-road/vehicle 6. gun/barrel 7. paper/cup 8. electric/windows 9. car/park 10. soup/bowl
Übung 75: 1. pushed 2. through 3. counter 4. brain 5. smiled 6. policemen 7. back
Übung 76: 1. a 2. b 3. c 4. a

Übung 77: 1. do something until the cows come home/etwas machen, bis man schwarz wird 2. hit the nail on the head/den Nagel auf den Kopf treffen 3. have a screw loose/eine Schraube locker haben 4. be in one's birthday suit/im Adamskostüm sein 5. throw a spanner in the works/einen Knüppel zwischen die Beine werfen

Übung 78: 1. shed 2. peered 3. yard 4. cursed 5. rake 6. appeared 7. noisily 8. crack

Übung 79: 1. out 2. into 3. up 4. to 5. up 6. in 7. out

Übung 80: 1. richtig 2. richtig 3. falsch 4. falsch 5. richtig 6. richtig 7. falsch

Übung 81: 1. distance/Entfernung 2. speed/Geschwindigkeit 3. mirror/Spiegel 4. fraction/Bruchteil 5. aim/zielen 6. brake/Bremse 7. hole/Loch 8. step/treten 9. bang/Knall 10. steering wheel/Lenkrad

Übung 82: 1. slowly 2. hated 3. unlocked 4. light 5. disagreed 6. alive 7. unlikely 8. right

Übung 83: 1. b 2. c 3. b

Übung 84: 1. falsch 2. richtig 3. falsch 4. falsch 5. richtig 6. falsch

Übung 85: 1. run 2. straight 3. call 4. whisper 5. calm 6. butt

Übung 86: 1. hospital 2. spy 3. clothes 4. interrupt 5. amazed 6. casualty 7. smile 8. envelope 9. change Lösung: operation

Übung 87: 1. He drove along the road quickly. 2. Hunter turned into a side street. 3. They immediately went to casualty. 4. Could you lend me 10 pounds? 5. They hugged each other briefly. 6. She returned with an envelope in her hand.

Übung 88: 1. heard 2. hugged 3. swore 4. tried 5. approached 6. bit 7. stabbed 8. thought 9. threw

Übung 89: 1. tightly 2. silence 3. everywhere 4. stopped 5. went off 6. standing 7. pretty 8. narrow

Übung 90: 1. handbag 2. thief 3. stupid 4. narrow 5. sunglasses 6. reinforcements 7. embarrassing

Übung 91: 1. b 2. a 3. c 4. c

Übung 92: 1. richtig 2. reinforcement 3. richtig 4. richtig 5. spontaneously 6. receive 7. richtig 8. embarrassing

Übung 93: 1. forget 2. disappear 3. spray 4. interrupt 5. whisper 6. order 7. promise

Übung 94: 1. shelves 2. people 3. copies 4. potatoes 5. mice 6. boxes 7. teeth

Übung 95: 1. on 2. in 3. around 4. down 5. along 6. from 7. around 8. along 9. on

Übung 96: 1. returned 2. screamed 3. waited 4. angry 5. jumped 6. saw 7. reached

Übung 97: 1. crate 2. pat 3. packet 4. carton 5. tub 6. loaf 7. tin

Übung 98: 1. worst 2. more important 3. better 4. prettier 5. simpler 6. more tired 7. more dangerous

Übung 99: 1. falsch 2. richtig 3. falsch 4. richtig 5. richtig 6. falsch 7. richtig

Übung 100: 1. c, h, m 2. b, d, j 3. a, f, k, o 4. e, g, n 5. i, l, p

Übung 101: 1. search 2. crawled 3. screamed 4. pain 5. immediately 6. struggled 7. shot 8. rubbed

Übung 102: 1. Hunter's gun 2. the gangsters' hideout 3. people's lives 4. Callaghan's office 5. Martin and Julia's flat 6. children's toys 7. the plane's wheels

Übung 103: 1. attack 2. mix 3. develop 4. enter 5. dark 6. repeat 7. sample 8. second 9. straight Lösung: kidnapper

Übung 104: 1. company/headquarters 2. gun/barrel 3. cocktail/shaker 4. card/table 5. bottle/opener 6. organic/food 7. business/partner 8. human/shield 9. special/delivery

Übung 105: 1. panicked 2. started 3. needed 4. arrested 5. came 6. limped 7. said 8. thanked

Übung 106: 1. Verband 2. beschimpfen 3. verletzt 4. Stirn 5. zusammenbrechen 6. zielen 7. verwirrt

Übung 107: 1. middleman 2. surprised 3. healthy 4. sealed 5. poisoned 6. lethal 7. grinned 8. liquid

Übung 108: 1. richtig 2. falsch 3. falsch 4. falsch 5. richtig 6. falsch 7. richtig

Übung 109: 1. Well done! 2. "Tertechs" was developed as a biological weapon in the 1980s. 3. The company was almost bankrupt. 4. When he was young, he wanted to be a policeman. 5. Callaghan pretended that she didn't know Turner.

Übung 110: 1. In the Pacific. 2. In the flavour sachet in Mealomeal products. 3. No. 4. His leg. 5. At the police academy.

Lösungen Abschlusstest

Übung 1: 1. hurry 2. repeat 3. apologise 4. spin round 5. disappear 6. crawl 7. look

Übung 2: 1. dealer 2. practise 3. impossible 4. injury 5. padlock 6. jealous 7. guaranteed

Übung 3: 1. c 2. b 3. b 4. a

Übung 4: 1. decide 2. hurry 3. pumpkin 4. little 5. order 6. grenade 7. farmyard 8. agree 9. wave Lösung: espionage

Übung 5: 1. The plane took off fast. 2. Hunter went out of the room fast. Can I borrow 25 pounds from you? 4. Hunter was the best agent in the secret service.

Übung 6: 1. speak 2. tell 3. press 4. wear 5. loose 6. fan

Übung 7: 1. took 2. waited 3. came 4. became 5. was 6. carried on 7. looked 8. ducked 9. spoke 10. leapt

Übung 8: 1. Section 3, Dr Wander's Laboratory Unit. 2. Explosives and wood shavings. 3. With a rake. 4. The trouser he bought for her were too big. 5. In the neck.

Übung 9: 1. Hunter said it would be too risky to break in with Agnes. 2. The plane flew back to England immediately. 3. Do I look like an idiot? 4. The guard threw a grenade and blew up the car. 5. Callaghan had known Turner since the police academy.

Übung 10: 1. inconvenient 2. richtig 3. richtig 4. casualty 5. happiness 6. richtig 7. intelligence

Übung 11: 1. distance/Entfernung 2. speed/Geschwindigkeit 3. mirror/Spiegel 4. fraction/Bruchteil 5. aim/zielen 6. brake/Bremse 7. hole/Loch 8. step/treten 9. bang/Knall 10. steering wheel/Lenkrad